THE QUINTESSENTIAL CAST IRON COOKBOOK

100 One-Pan Recipes to Make the Most of Your Skillet

HOWIE SOUTHWORTH and GREG MATZA

Wall Street Journal **bestselling authors**

Skyhorse Publishing

Skyhorse Publishing books may be purchased in bulk at special discounts for sales promotion, corporate gifts, fund-raising, or educational purposes. Special editions can also be created to specifications. For details, contact the Special Sales Department, Skyhorse Publishing, 307 West 36th Street, 11th Floor, New York, NY 10018 or info@skyhorsepublishing.com.

Skyhorse® and Skyhorse Publishing® are registered trademarks of Skyhorse Publishing, Inc.®, a Delaware corporation.

Visit our website at www.skyhorsepublishing.com.

10 9 8 7 6 5 4 3 2 1

Library of Congress Cataloging-in-Publication Data is available on file.

Cover design by Qualcom
Cover photo by Howie Southworth

Print ISBN: 978-1-5107-4248-2
Ebook ISBN: 978-1-5107-4253-6

Printed in China

TABLE OF CONTENTS

WHAT MAKES A CAST-IRON SKILLET SO LOVABLE?

Let's face it. If your kitchen had just one pan, one single tool to accomplish any cooking concoction of which you dare to dream, it should be a pretty awesome one, right? The chosen one, the golden child, the king of the ring, the one true pan to rule them all! It should be a cast-iron skillet! Cast iron has been used for cooking since the Han Dynasty in China. That's more than 2,000 years of skillet cornbread! Well, perhaps not cornbread specifically, but you get the idea. Cast-iron cookware is a proven hero, never goes out of style, and cannot be destroyed, despite how you feel about yourself as a home cook.

Now that you've given in to our hype and acquired a skillet of this magic material, here's a pat on the back in the form of our top eleven reasons why you've made an incredibly good decision:

1. **It is virtually indestructible.** When cooking with a nonstick pan, you're advised not to use metal implements. Heck, sometimes you're even told not to use a wooden spoon! What gives? Free the spatula! This skillet will not scratch, so you can use any type of cooking utensil. Throw away the worries with cast iron. "But I need a nonstick surface," you say? Once a skillet is properly seasoned, the skillet becomes nonstick. And that nonstick gets non-stickier the more you use it. Ta-da!

2. **It can be used on any heat source.** Unless you're trying to cook in a small forge in the garage, cast iron cannot be destroyed. It can go from a gas or electric stovetop to the oven and back again without skipping a beat. Even over the campfire, you ask? Absolutely. In fact, we've dedicated a whole chapter to outdoor cookin'!

3. **It retains heat like no other cooking vessel.** Keeping food warm ahead of a meal no longer requires a low-temperature oven or flame. Has Thanksgiving prep got your kitchen in a tornado-like state? At least your andouille cornbread dressing is nice and toasty at the table instead of taking up valuable oven room. Freedom!

4. **In a word: Browning.** Have you ever heard the now ubiquitous phrase, "Golden, brown, and delicious" or "GBD"? That's one of the hallmarks of cast-iron cooking.

Since you'll experience consistent heat on every surface, your steaks will have that to-die-for sear, your crispy hash browns will rival any greasy spoon, and your pineapple upside-down cake will have that luscious sheen you've only seen on television.

5. **It's very, very talented.** This book will show you how to sauté, shallow fry, deep fry, sear, bake, braise, stew, and even boil all in one piece of hardware. Specialized kitchens use seven different devices for what you can accomplish with just one cast-iron dream machine. She's the best multitasker money can buy. Speaking of which . . .

6. **It's cheap.** Your first cast-iron skillet will set you back about $20, compared to an acceptable entry–level, aluminum-clad sauté pan at $100. Since you can use cast iron to do everything mentioned in #5 above, you might have a single vessel in your arsenal, but you'll be able to produce myriad dishes for less than half the cost of a night out at the movies! OK, you still have to buy ingredients, but you get the point!

7. **It provides a bit of a workout.** Cast-iron cooking is terrific exercise. The skillet is heavy; moving it from stovetop to oven can work the biceps, deltoids, and, depending on where your oven is, the glutes. We kid, but the truth is you hardly ever have to move the skillet during cooking, and accidental tipping of the pan is almost impossible. It does get hot, and keeps heat well. Always wear a shirt, especially when frying!

8. **Cleanup is a piece of cake.** (Before you even ask, of course you can bake a cake in a cast-iron skillet.) If your dish doesn't simply slide out of the pan and bits of food are left behind, they will easily lift off. In the case of particularly sticky fare, a bit of stiff brush action, water, and wiping will usually do the trick. Over time and use, a coating (a.k.a. the seasoning or patina) is developed on the inside of the pan that helps "slicker the slickness."

9. **It's low fat.** As mentioned above, with repeated use cast iron will develop a coating that acts like the (ahem, inferior) nonstick coating of "nonstick" pans. This means that over time you'll use less oil to cook. In some cases you may not even need oil at all to obtain a perfect sear, flawless stir-fries, or no-mess scrambles.

10. **It gives you superpowers.** Studies have shown that cast-iron cooking has a cool benefit of adding the iron you need directly into the dishes you cook. That's right! This book can help increase your immunity and give you energy!

11. **It's the gift that keeps on giving.** Cast-iron cookware has been known to pass between generations of family cooks. You are the beneficiary of the work your grandmother did in her cast-iron skillet. Your kids gain from years of seasoning in your kitchen, and so on down the road. It may just be the perfect wedding gift. The longer a cast-iron skillet remains in use, the more soul it gives to the latest dish. Every dish that is cooked in a well-loved cast-iron skillet owes a bit of its spirit and depth to every dish that came before. Be a good person. Cook in cast iron.

A SIMPLE SKILLET-BUYING GUIDE

For once, the phrase, "You get what you pay for," works in your favor. When it comes to cast-iron skillets, the simple, inexpensive ones are the best. Still, there are a few questions to ask yourself before your purchase:

Where can I buy a cast-iron skillet?
This list may be surprising. Over the last two decades, cooking at home has exploded, hopefully only figuratively, due to TV cooking programs and food-related competition shows. Everyone seems to be getting into the cooking supply game.

- Rural lifestyle retailers
- Specialty retailers
- Outdoor lifestyle retailers
- Value retailers
- Hardware retailers
- Homeware retailers
- Kitchen supply retailers
- Department retailers
- Online mega-retailers

Enameled versus Non-enameled
When shopping for a cast-iron pan, you may run into several models with white and/or colored enamel on them. If the enamel is only on the outside of the pan, it won't impact the cooking. It'll make your pan significantly more expensive, but who are we to judge the cost of beauty.

If, however, the cooking surface of the pan is enameled, we think that it ceases to be a cast-iron skillet. The many notable benefits of using a cast-iron pan are directly attributable to the fact that the iron is in direct contact with the food. If there's a layer of ceramic between the iron and the food, you are no longer using cast iron.

Enameled pans are beautiful. They are great for long-cooking stews, and are generally a great addition to your kitchen. However, if you want to read about the best ways to use an enamel pan, you're reading the wrong book.

Seasoned versus Unseasoned

You can buy a cast-iron skillet that went through a seasoning process in the factory. In fact, the leading manufacturer of cast-iron skillets pre-seasons all of its new skillets. In theory, this means you can use the skillet right out of the box without taking the time and trouble to season it yourself. Pre-seasoned skillets, however, do cost a bit more.

So if you're the kind of person who likes do-it-yourself projects and saving money, try to find an unseasoned skillet, though it's increasingly difficult to find! If you want to use the skillet immediately, and the price difference is moot, go pre-seasoned.

For instructions on seasoning your raw skillet, see the "Seasoning, Cleaning, Repair and Care" section on page 10.

Sizes

Cast-iron pans come in a wide variety of sizes, from 2-inch-diameter novelties to 20-inch-diameter behemoths.

When buying your first skillet, your choice is highly dependent upon the size of your audience. If you're flying solo and are just getting your cooking feet wet (note: don't cook with your feet), perhaps an 8-inch-diameter skillet would suffice. However, once you start entertaining guests, your size needs change. A 10-inch-diameter skillet is great for small family meals. If you're cooking for a crowd, a 12-inch-diameter skillet is a must.

Another way to approach the size question is by looking through this book. The recipes include recommendations for skillet sizes. So, if you want to make every recipe in this book exactly as we made it, you can do so with three skillets: 8-inch, 10-inch, and 12-inch. You can also easily adjust any recipe in this book to fit the skillet you own.

Lids

Most skillets come without lids. We strongly recommend investing in a lid. Lids enable you to use your skillet for any dish that requires a long braise or simmer.

Specifically, a lid performs two duties. First, it keeps all the water in the pan. As you simmer, water evaporates, but when it hits that lid, it condenses and rains back in to the food. Second, that evaporation and rain keep the air above your braising liquid incredibly moist, protecting any meat or vegetables from turning to jerky.

If you don't have a lid, you can always improvise. We'll often use another skillet turned upside down, a lid from a nearby stock pot, or a piece of foil. These will work, but a lid that tightly fits your skillet will work better.

Vintage versus New

At its base, cast iron is cast iron. Whether manufactured in 1815 or 2015, it's fundamentally the same. The heating and browning properties of old versus new pans are identical.

That said, pans made after about 1950 are different. Over the years, there have been some manufacturing changes that have a subtle impact on your pan. Specifically:

- **Vintage skillets can be thinner and lighter.** Whether this is an advantage or liability is really a matter of taste. Vintage skillets are easier on the biceps, but less iron means less heat retention.
- **Vintage skillets are usually smoother.** Older manufacturing processes included a process called "smoothing." Remarkably enough, this resulted in a smooth pan surface. New pans are a bit bumpy, though they will smooth out with use and seasoning.
- **Vintage skillets may need new seasoning.** Vintage skillets, especially those that you can find at a garage sale, may not be in the best shape. It may take some time and effort to get them restored. See the "Seasoning, Cleaning, Repair, and Care" section on page 10.

So, buy what you prefer. Like loving ballet versus digging punk rock, vintage versus new is more a question of taste than some inherent value of the performance.

Pot Holders

Cast iron gets very, very hot. Invest in good pot holders and use them. If every recipe included every moment when we'd suggest using a pot holder around a hot skillet, this book would be roughly 600 pages longer than it is.

Our favorite potholders are thin suede. They aren't cheap, but they do a great job of providing maximal protection, without being too bulky. But really, most anything will work. Except wet towels. Don't try wet towels.

SEASONING, CLEANING, REPAIR, AND CARE

Initial Seasoning

If you've opted to purchase a pre-seasoned skillet, as will often be the case in this day and age, you may skip this step and get right to cooking. Then again, this is a good step to practice, to give the factory seasoning a personal boost. It's also useful if you ever need to reboot after some Herculean scrubbing.

What do we mean by seasoning? We're not talking about cumin or paprika here. We're discussing kick-starting that lovely coating that will continue to naturally build on the skillet and improve every time you cook. The more seasoning your skillet develops, the more nonstick properties it provides.

Over time, the initially pebbly surface of the raw skillet will become smooth as ice. You can season a skillet very simply using these steps:

- Heat oven to 350°F, arranging one rack in the center of your oven and another rack below it.
- Make sure that the skillet is completely clean. Use a nylon pad, nylon brush, or salt as a scouring agent.
- Wipe moisture off the skillet and then place over high heat on the stovetop. Heat until any remaining moisture has evaporated, usually 2–4 minutes.
- Using a towel, apply a uniform, thin coat of oil (any cooking oil is fine) to the surface you want seasoned. This can be just the bottom of the pan, or it can include the exterior.
- Place a baking sheet on the lower rack of your oven.
- Place the skillet, upside down, on the upper rack, above the baking sheet. The baking sheet is there to catch any drips.
- Cook for about 1 hour.

This process may be repeated as often as necessary, or if you're bored and want to do something nice for your skillet. If you've got an hour to kill, only good can come from this. In the case of an inherited and fairly battered or rusty old skillet, repeated seasoning will be necessary to get it back into peak, shiny, blackened condition.

Cleaning

Throughout this book we use many different cooking methods, from stir frying and sautéing to baking and braising. Most recipes will leave the inside of the skillet more or less clear of tough bits. There will be times, however, that you have caked-on egg to resolve, or an undesired layer of slightly more than crisp rice to mitigate. Do not fret.

Live by this haiku, and you will have a pan that lasts for generations.

> *Long soak is evil*
> *Keep the wet quick in your pan*
> *Oil is your friend*

You can probably drop your skillet down an elevator shaft without harming it, but leave it to soak overnight and you're in for some serious trouble. Why? Because iron rusts. And your cast-iron pan is, oddly enough, made of iron.

You may, however, soak the skillet for the minimum amount of time it will take to cleanly scrape off tough bits. For example, I've made the Creamy, Chewy Mac and Cheese recipe dozens of times. About half of those ended with some crusty cheese seemingly soldered to the inside of the skillet. Filling the inside of a warm skillet with water for 15 minutes makes it easy to brush the stuck stuff away.

Common sense and the handy haiku are probably enough. But, just in case you're the kind of person who likes specific instructions, here is the recommended process for cleaning and caring for your pan:

1. **Clean your pan with running water and a nonmetallic brush or scraper**. Nylon pads or brushes work great. Bamboo scrapers work even better. For harder, burned-on grit, a brief soak plus a good scrape should do the trick. Every once in a while, a soapy sponge may be used, but it's not typically necessary. Soap will eat away at your seasoning, so be judicious.
2. **Heat dry your pan immediately after cleaning**. Allowing the skillet to drip dry or simply wiping with a towel is not good enough. Even a small amount of

moisture will cause rust. The best practice is to heat your pan over a high flame until all the water has evaporated.

3. **Oil to protect your pan.** Once the water has evaporated, drizzle some cooking oil in the skillet and spread it evenly with a paper towel. Allow it to heat just until it starts smoking. This will, over time, improve your seasoning. This coating of oil also protects the skillet from those dastardly water molecules.

Repair

Let's say that you "accidentally" soaked your skillet overnight, or perhaps you got distracted and forgot to fully dry the skillet on the stove. Now you have rust—evil, awful, red rust.

The first step is admitting that you have a problem. The next step is to approach a clergy member of your choice for redemption from the sin of harming cast iron. The final step—and hopefully the easiest one—is repair.

Follow this handy guide for repairing rusty spots or bringing an adopted vintage pan back from the dead:

- **Wipe with an oiled towel.** Most rust is simply on the surface. Take a paper or cloth towel; pour a bit of oil on it; and rub, rub, rub. I haven't yet summoned a genie, but I have dismissed quite a few rust spots. Then, clean the skillet as you would after cooking. If the rust persists after you heat dry, the problem is deeper.
- **Scrub with steel wool or coarse salt.** Scrubbing the rust with fine steel wool (like an S.O.S® pad) or a few tablespoons of kosher or sea salt will scrape away the offending bits of surface iron and typically get rid of the problem. However, this will also eat away at the seasoning on the skillet. Perform the initial seasoning process from page 10.
- **Buy a new skillet.** There is a point of no return for a cast-iron skillet. Although we've never personally experienced this, we've heard some horror stories of disfigured skillets that needed more than the makeovers suggested above. Lodge Manufacturing, the largest manufacturer of cast-iron skillets in North America, recommends taking the skillet to a machine shop and having it sandblasted back to raw iron. In truth, this seems like getting body work done on your Pinto. Given that you can buy a brand new pan for the cost of this book, we recommend shelling out for a new skillet.

EARLY INSPIRATION

SPINACH AND CHEDDAR FRITTATA

TOTAL TIME: 30 minutes

EQUIPMENT: 10-inch skillet

SERVES: 4–6

INGREDIENTS:

2 Tbsp extra virgin olive oil

1 small onion, peeled and diced

1 bag (6 oz) baby spinach

8 large eggs

1 tsp salt

½ tsp black pepper

8 oz sharp cheddar cheese, shredded

> I've never been good at folding an omelet. I'm not alone in this flaw. (You know who you are.) So, when I discovered that the Italians don't even bother with the folding, my life changed completely. I love frittatas! All the awesomeness of an omelet without the darned folding. Sorry, France!
>
> —Howie

Preheat the oven to 375°F. Add the olive oil to your skillet and heat over medium. Once the oil begins to shimmer, add the onion to the skillet. Sauté until the onion is translucent, about 6–8 minutes. Add half the spinach to the skillet and stir it into the onion. The spinach will wilt quickly. Add the other half of the spinach and wilt once again. This will take 3–4 minutes.

Lower the heat to medium-low. In a large mixing bowl, whisk together the eggs, salt, pepper, and cheese. Immediately pour the well-mixed egg mixture into the skillet. Using a rubber spatula, gently stir the egg mixture to incorporate the spinach and onion. Leave the skillet over medium-low heat until small bubbles come to the surface regularly, about 6–8 minutes. This is how you'll know the bottom crust is forming.

Transfer the skillet to the oven and bake for 10 minutes, or until the frittata gets "puffy." Once you remove the skillet from the oven, the frittata will seem to deflate. Let it cool to room temperature. You may serve directly from the skillet, or shake the skillet to assure the bottom has released, and then slide the frittata onto a plate for cutting and serving.

PHILADELPHIA EGG PUFF

TOTAL TIME: 1 hour, 15 minutes

EQUIPMENT: 8-inch skillet

SERVES: 3–4

INGREDIENTS:

1 sheet frozen puff pastry

Flour, for dusting

4 oz block of cream cheese, cubed

8 oz nova salmon lox or smoked salmon, diced

4 scallions, thinly sliced

6 large eggs

1 cup half and half or cream

½ tsp salt

½ tsp ground black pepper

Like the namesake cream cheese, this quiche has nothing to do with the city of Philadelphia. But back in 1880, when the New York farmer who created the cheese was trying to sell it, saying that something was from Philly was calling it the height of class. Clearly, it was a time before the Rocky movies.

—Greg

Remove puff pastry sheet from the freezer and allow to thaw, folded on the counter, for about 30 minutes.

Preheat the oven to 425°F. Dust your counter or board with flour, unfold the puff pastry and place the sheet atop the flour, and dust with some more flour. Roll the sheet into a 10-inch square, smoothing out all the fold seams.

Transfer the pastry to your skillet, letting it settle into the bottom and along the sides. (This may take some manual encouragement.) Trim the corner edges, but make sure the pastry fills the skillet like a pie crust.

Place the cream cheese cubes along the bottom of the pastry shell in one layer. Next, add the salmon in one layer, and top with the scallions. In a large mixing bowl, whisk together the remaining ingredients. Pour the mixture into the pastry shell slowly, trying not to disturb the cream cheese, salmon, and scallions. The scallions may wish to float, and that's OK.

Bake in the oven for 20–25 minutes, or until the edges of the pastry are golden brown. Allow the puff to cool on the counter for at least 20 minutes. Cut into wedges. It can be served warm, but it's better at room temperature.

PESTO CHICKEN SCRAMBLE

TOTAL TIME: 15 minutes

EQUIPMENT: 10- or 12-inch skillet

SERVES: 4

INGREDIENTS:

3 Tbsp salted butter

1 cup leftover cooked chicken, cut into bite-size chunks

½ cup cream

8 eggs

¼ cup pesto (bought, or see below for recipe)

> If you've ever wondered what to do with the leftover wing and half-thigh from last night's rotisserie chicken, this is the answer. And, yes, that's a lot of butter, but don't skimp. Butter makes food taste good.
>
> —Greg

Heat butter in a skillet over medium-high heat. When butter begins to brown and smell nutty, turn down heat to medium and add chicken. Toss the chicken to cover in butter and sauté until the edges of the chicken start to brown (3–4 minutes).

Meanwhile, put the eggs and cream in a blender. Blend at a high speed for 1 minute. (I know, the blender is loud, and it's another thing to clean, but getting the eggs all frothed up will be worth it.)

Pour the eggs into the skillet. Using a rubber spatula, gently fold the eggs, sliding the cooked egg toward you, allowing the liquid egg to fall to the skillet. Continue gently folding until the eggs are nearly done, about 2–3 minutes.

Fold the pesto into the egg and chicken mixture. Continue cooking until fragrant, about 20–30 seconds.

Remove from the pan and serve immediately.

PESTO

INGREDIENTS:

3 Tbsp pine (or other) nuts

1 cup basil leaves

2 small cloves garlic, roughly chopped

¼ cup Parmesan cheese

¼ cup olive oil

½ tsp salt

> Pesto is a very forgiving sauce, so don't stress about exact amounts or substitutions. If you don't have pine nuts, substitute any roasted nut, like pistachios or walnuts, or skip them entirely. If it tastes bitter, that's just because the basil didn't get quite enough sun while it was growing. Add a sprinkle of sugar and salt and you're good to go.
>
> —Greg

Toast the nuts in a medium-hot dry skillet until fragrant and slightly browned, about 3 minutes. Note that the nuts will go from white to burned very quickly, so pay attention to them and take them out of the skillet as soon as you see them start to brown.

Add all ingredients to a blender or food processor and blend until smooth.

MANCHEGO AND MUSHROOM SPANISH TORTILLA

TOTAL TIME: 1 hour, 10 minutes

EQUIPMENT: 10 inch skillet

SERVES: 6–8

"You mean those flat bready things we use to make tacos?" Nope. A Spanish "tortilla" is closer to an omelet or a frittata than a taco. "Tortilla" actually means a small cake, and even though this is a far cry from angel food, it kinda looks like a cake. Honestly, I don't really know why they hold onto the confusing name, but it's delicious.

—Howie

INGREDIENTS:

5 Tbsp extra virgin olive oil

1 small onion, diced

6 oz cremini, white button, or shiitake mushrooms, stemmed and thinly sliced

1½ tsp salt, divided

½ tsp ground black pepper

8 large eggs

6 oz manchego cheese, shredded

¼ cup flat leaf parsley, roughly chopped

Preheat the oven to 375°F. In the skillet, heat the oil over medium heat, and then add the onion and mushrooms, along with ½ teaspoon of salt and ½ teaspoon of pepper. Sauté until the onions are translucent and the mushrooms lose their water and begin to brown, about 6–8 minutes.

In a large mixing bowl, whisk together the eggs, 1 teaspoon of salt, cheese, and parsley. Whisk vigorously, then gently pour into the skillet, trying to keep the mushrooms and onions against the bottom of the pan.

After about 3 minutes, test the edges of the skillet with a rubber spatula to see if they've begun to set. Run the spatula around the edge of the tortilla—between the egg and the pan—to encourage the edges to come away from the sides of the skillet. After about 5 minutes, you should be able to partially lift to check if the bottom is set. Once the bottom is set, transfer the skillet to the oven and bake for 20 minutes. Test for doneness by gently shaking the skillet. If the middle of the tortilla is still liquidy, bake for an additional 2–4 minutes, until the middle is more firm.

Allow the tortilla to cool in the skillet for a half hour. Then, place a plate upside down on top of the skillet. Hold the plate firmly against the skillet and carefully flip the skillet over, releasing the tortilla onto the plate. Cut into wedges and serve with a dollop of sour cream.

PERFECT HASH BROWNS

TOTAL TIME: 25 minutes

EQUIPMENT: 8-inch skillet

SERVES: 2-4

INGREDIENTS:

2 tsp extra virgin olive oil

2 tsp salted butter

½ tsp salt, divided

12-oz russet or Yukon
    Gold potato, peeled and
    shredded

When I was a kid, I loved pancakes. But I never ordered them. Why? Because my Mom insisted that I couldn't order hash browns with them. "It's two starches!" she would proclaim, as if that were a problem. Now that I'm making my own breakfasts, I can starch it up to my heart's content. The only problem is that everyone within smelling range of these crispy, buttery HBs insists that I share. Life is so difficult.

—Greg

Heat oil and butter in the skillet over medium-low heat. When the butter melts, swirl the pan to combine the oil and butter. Sprinkle ¼ teaspoon of salt across the bottom of the skillet. Then, drop shreds of potato evenly across the bottom of the skillet, until you have no shreds left. With a rubber spatula, gently form the shredded potato into an even disc. Try not to overly compress the potato; you're simply looking to form a flat, even layer, and want it to remain airy inside. Sprinkle the remaining ¼ teaspoon of salt across the top of the potato layer.

After ten minutes, gently lift up one side of the hash brown to check that the bottom is golden brown and releases easily from the bottom of the skillet. Shake the skillet to see that the hash brown freely shuffles back and forth.

It is best to try and flip the hash brown completely in one fluid motion using only one hand on the skillet handle. If you cannot or will not attempt this (it takes practice), you may use one spatula below the hash brown and flip it like a pancake.

After ten more minutes, this hash brown is perfect and can be moved to a plate, cut up or torn into by hungry eaters. Psst . . . I drizzle maple syrup on mine. Shhh.

CORNED BEEF HASH

TOTAL TIME: 35 minutes

EQUIPMENT: 10-inch skillet

SERVES: 4-6

INGREDIENTS:

1 Tbsp unsalted butter

1 tsp extra virgin olive oil

1 medium russet potato, diced

1 small red onion, diced

8 oz sliced corned beef, shredded

½ tsp salt

½ tsp ground black pepper

1 Tbsp heavy cream

I grew up in New Jersey, and therefore judge a diner by its corned beef hash with two eggs, scrambled soft, and some rye toast with lots of butter. In fact, if I'm with my co-author Greg, he always asks the server if he could order his butter on my toast. Dry rye? Who does that? Anyhow, this is my ode to the New Jersey diner, by which you may judge this book. Also, please judge Greg.

—Howie

Heat the skillet over medium-low heat and add the butter and oil. When the butter has melted, add the potatoes and onions to the skillet and sauté until the potatoes begin to brown at the edges, about 5 minutes. Add the corned beef, salt, and pepper to the skillet and stir through the onions and potatoes. Allow the mixture to sit, undisturbed for 5 minutes, then stir again, scraping the bottom from the skillet to pick up any browned bits.

Allow to sit for another 5 minutes and repeat the scraping and stirring. Do this one more time for 5 minutes. Scrape again and mix in the heavy cream. Allow the mixture to thicken slightly, about 2 minutes. Serve with eggs made to order and rye toast *with lots of butter*. Take that, Greg!

CRISPY, FLAKY BISCUITS

TOTAL TIME: 35 minutes

EQUIPMENT: 12-inch skillet

SERVES: 8–12

INGREDIENTS:

3 cups all-purpose flour

4 tsp baking powder

1 tsp baking soda

1½ Tbsp sugar

1 tsp salt

¾ cup unsalted butter, cold, cut into ¼-inch cubes

1¼ cups buttermilk

2 Tbsp extra virgin olive oil

Biscuits. What can one say? To me, it's become critical to use a cast-iron skillet to make these biscuits. Especially since most of them will rise along the sides of the skillet and that contact makes for an even more delicious crispy exterior! Lightly snappy on the outside, layers of creamy cloud on the inside. Biscuits.

—Howie

Preheat oven to 400°F. In a large mixing bowl, whisk together the flour, baking soda, baking powder, sugar, and salt. Add the butter cubes and incorporate into the flour mixture with a pastry cutter or squeeze with your fingertips until the pieces of butter are consistently smaller than peas. Add the buttermilk and quickly mix well with your hands, until dough forms. This whole mixing process should be completed as fast as possible—at most 2 minutes—in order to avoid melting all the butter.

Dust the counter or a board with flour and transfer your dough from the bowl. Dust the top of the dough with more flour and begin to flatten with your hand or a floured rolling pin. Roll the dough until it is ¾-inch thick. Drizzle 1 tablespoon of oil in the skillet. Cut out dough rounds with a 2-inch biscuit cutter or the top of a 2-inch wide glass, and place the dough rounds into the bottom of the skillet, first around the edges, and then the middle. Drizzle remaining tablespoon of oil over the tops of the biscuits.

Bake until biscuits are starting to brown, about 20–25 minutes. Serve the biscuits warm with Mixed Berry Jam from page 33, Creamy Country Gravy from page 31, honey, or butter!

CREAMY COUNTRY GRAVY

TOTAL TIME: 35 minutes

EQUIPMENT: 12-inch skillet

SERVES: 8–10

INGREDIENTS:

¼ cup extra virgin olive oil

¼ cup unsalted butter

½ lb raw chorizo, or other pork
   sausage, casings removed

½ cup all-purpose flour

6 cups milk

½ tsp ground cayenne pepper

½ tsp salt

> When I was 12, I took a road trip from New Jersey to Ohio with my mom to visit friends, Midwest transplants from the Deep South. When we arrived, there were fresh-out-of-the-oven biscuits and what appeared to be creamy sausage on the stove. My curiosity was piqued. Our host served me up a toasty split biscuit and smothered it with this magical sausage sauce! My life changed that day, my friends.
>
> —Howie

Heat butter and oil over medium heat. Once the butter melts, add sausage to the skillet. Cook the sausage until slightly browned, about 5 minutes, breaking apart the sausage as it cooks. Sprinkle flour over the sausage and mix. Sauté this mixture for 2 minutes, then slowly stir in the milk, salt, and cayenne. Continue to stir the mixture until it comes to a boil.

Lower the heat to medium-low and allow the gravy to simmer, stirring occasionally, until it reaches the desired wavy gravy consistency, about 8 minutes. Remove from the heat and serve immediately with fresh Crispy, Flaky Biscuits from page 29.

MIXED BERRY JAM

TOTAL TIME: 25 minutes

EQUIPMENT: 8-inch skillet

SERVES: 6–8

INGREDIENTS:

4 cups mixed berries
(raspberries, blackberries,
blueberries, strawberries,
etc.)

½ cup white sugar

> It's early Sunday morning and all you want
> is your paper, a cuppa Joe, and the sound of
> your kids clamoring for hot jam to cease. This
> awesome addition to any morning routine will
> not only satisfy the household beasts, but once
> you figure out how simple it is, you may even
> keep a secret stash for yourself!
>
> —Howie

Pre-heat the skillet over medium-low. Mix the berries and sugar in a mixing bowl. With a potato masher or large fork, mash the berries with the sugar until the berries begin to break down and juices are released.

Place this mixture in the heated skillet and bring to an active simmer, stirring frequently. Allow to boil down for 12–15 minutes, or until it begins to thicken to a pancake-syrup consistency. Pour the jam out of the skillet into a serving bowl.

Serve with Crispy, Flaky Biscuits from page 29, warm toast, pancakes, waffles, crepes, or just a spoon.

JOHNNY CAKES

TOTAL TIME: 15 minutes

EQUIPMENT: 12-inch skillet

SERVES: 4-6

INGREDIENTS:

1½ cups milk

2 Tbsp sugar

1 Tbsp extra virgin olive oil

1 large egg

½ cup all-purpose flour

1 cup cornmeal

1 tsp baking powder

1 tsp salt

2-3 Tbsp butter

Do you remember *The Sopranos*? I do. Vito Spatafore was bestowed the adorable nickname of Johnny Cakes after falling in love with this New England staple (and the burly cook who whipped them up). You're about to fall for them as well. The food, not the cook. Then again, you can love me, too. Smooch!

—Greg

Preheat the oven to 200°F. In a microwave safe bowl, warm the milk in the microwave for 45 seconds. Stir the sugar into the milk to dissolve. Whisk the oil and egg into the milk mixture.

In a separate bowl, whisk together the flour, cornmeal, baking powder, and salt. Add the milk mixture to the dry ingredients and stir together. Only stir until everything is barely combined (no flour streaks). Some lumps are OK. It makes for a fluffier johnny cake!

Melt 1 tablespoon of butter in the skillet over medium heat. Using a ⅓ cup measure, drop batter in rough circles into the pan. Don't fry more than 4 cakes at a time. After about 1½ minutes you should see tiny bubbles appear on top of the batter. Flip the cakes with a spatula. After about one more minute, remove the cakes and keep them in a warm oven on a plate or baking sheet while you fry the rest.

Add more butter to the pan and fry additional cakes until you run out of batter. Serve warm with maple syrup.

OH YES, MORNING DOUGHNUTS

TOTAL TIME: 1 hour

EQUIPMENT: 8-inch skillet

SERVES: 4–6

INGREDIENTS:

2 Tbsp butter

½ cup plus 1 Tbsp sugar

½ cup milk

1 egg

1 cup all-purpose flour

2 tsp baking powder

¼ tsp salt

½ tsp plus 1 Tbsp cinnamon

3–4 cups canola or vegetable oil

> When it comes to doughnuts, I'm a traditionalist. I avoid the overly sweet crullers and maple bars, and I steer wide of fads like bacon glazes and pet rocks. To my taste, they are all inferior to the original—a humble, fried cake dough rolled in a bit of sugar and cinnamon. Once you've tasted these, you may never go back.
>
> —Greg

In a microwave safe bowl, place the butter and ½ cup of the sugar. Microwave on high for 45 seconds or until the butter melts completely. Set the bowl aside to cool slightly. In a separate bowl, whisk together the milk and eggs. In a large mixing bowl, whisk together the flour, baking powder, salt, and ½ teaspoon of the cinnamon.

Stir both bowlfuls of wet ingredients into the dry mixture until a dough forms. You may use a stand mixer with the dough hook attached. Cover the dough and place in the refrigerator for 30 minutes, up to an hour.

Turn the dough out onto a lightly floured counter or cutting board. Using a rolling pin, roll the dough to about ½-inch thick. Using a knife or pizza cutter, cut the dough into 1-inch squares.

Pour enough oil in the skillet to about 1 inch in depth. Heat the oil to 360°F over medium heat. If you do not have a thermometer, one handy trick is to use a wooden chopstick, like the kind you get with Chinese takeout. As the oil heats, touch the tip of the chopstick to the bottom of the skillet at an angle. Once you see bubbles forming around the entirety of the submerged chopstick, the oil is ready.

Prepare a wire rack over a baking sheet and place next to the stove. Combine remaining 1 tablespoon sugar and 1 tablespoon cinnamon in a wide shallow bowl and place next to the wire rack. Carefully place 6–8 dough squares into the hot oil at a time.

Flip each square when the bottom becomes golden brown, about 1½ minutes. After another minute the bottom should be golden brown, and they can be removed to the wire rack. Repeat until the dough squares have all been fried.

While the doughnuts are still hot, roll each in the cinnamon sugar and then back on the wire rack until all doughnuts are done. Serve warm with chocolate sauce, jam, or simply a cup of coffee.

FRUIT-STUFFED FRENCH TOAST

TOTAL TIME: 35 minutes

EQUIPMENT: 12-inch skillet

SERVES: 6

Growing up, I was amazed by French toast and even more intrigued by what a French toaster must look like. I'm glad I figured it out.

—Howie

INGREDIENTS:

4 eggs

1 cup milk

½ tsp granulated sugar

½ tsp salt

½ tsp vanilla extract

6 oz cream cheese, room temperature

3 oz greek-style yogurt

1 cup blueberries, blackberries, raspberries, or a mix, slightly mashed

12 slices (½ inch) white, sourdough or whole wheat bread

6 Tbsp butter, divided

Powdered sugar and maple syrup

Preheat the oven to 200°F. In a mixing bowl, whisk together eggs, milk, sugar, salt, and vanilla extract. Pour this mixture into a rimmed baking pan or a wide, shallow bowl. In a separate mixing bowl, combine the cream cheese, yogurt, and berries.

On half of the bread slices, spread about ⅓-½ cup of the cream cheese mixture, leaving a small gap between the spread and edge of the bread. Create a sandwich by topping each with a bare slice of bread, pressing gently to assure that it is firmly stuck together.

Prepare a wire rack over a rimmed baking sheet next to the stove. Heat 2 tablespoons of the butter in a skillet over medium-low heat. As the butter melts, take the first two sandwiches and dip each side into the egg mixture for about 8 seconds.

When the butter is just starting to brown, place the first two sandwiches in the skillet. Cook each side until golden brown, 2–3 minutes. Remove the sandwich to the wire rack and repeat to finish all of the sandwiches, adding more butter to the pan, as necessary

Once all the sandwiches have been fried, place the wire rack and baking sheet in the oven for 10 minutes. Remove and dust the top of the French toast with powdered sugar. Serve with warm maple syrup.

THE SUPER POPOVER

TOTAL TIME: 30 minutes

EQUIPMENT: 10-inch skillet

SERVES: 4–6

INGREDIENTS:

4 large eggs, room temperature

½ cup half-and-half, room temperature

½ tsp salt

½ tsp ground black pepper

½ cup all-purpose flour

2 Tbsp flat leaf parsley, roughly chopped

1½ cups asiago cheese, shredded

1 Tbsp extra virgin olive oil

1 Tbsp butter

I don't eat steak. I know, I know, I've heard it all, but calm down. I *do* like steakhouses! The reason: their bread! There's this classic joint in Washington, DC that serves—as their standard bread basket—gruyere popovers. Oversized, hollow, gooey pull-apart fantasy rolls! I'm making myself hungry just writing about them. With this recipe you can make them even bigger and sharable (or not).

—Howie

Place the clean, dry skillet in the oven and preheat to 400°F. In a mixing bowl, whisk together the eggs, half-and-half, salt, and pepper. Then whisk in the flour and you should have something resembling pancake batter. Add the parsley and cheese and mix through with a spoon.

Once the oven and skillet reach 400°F, carefully remove the skillet from the oven. Add the oil and butter to the skillet, and it will melt together within a few moments. Pour the batter into the skillet and return it to the oven for 20 minutes. At the 20 minute mark, the popover will have expanded like a balloon.

Carefully remove the skillet from the oven and serve directly to the table. It may deflate completely, but as folks tear hunks off of the popover, aromatic steam will emerge from the middle. It's a beautiful thing.

CHOCOLATE CHIP CREAM CHEESE COFFEE CAKE

TOTAL TIME: 1 hour, 25 minutes

EQUIPMENT: 8-inch skillet

SERVES: 4–6

INGREDIENTS:

Crumb Topping:

½ cup all-purpose flour

½ cup sugar

½ tsp ground cinnamon

¼ tsp salt

¼ cup cold unsalted butter, cut into ½ inch cubes

Cake Batter:

2 cups cake flour

1 tsp baking powder

¼ tsp baking soda

¼ tsp salt

8 oz cream cheese, softened

1 cup unsalted butter, softened

1¼ cups sugar

2 large eggs

¼ cup milk

12 oz mini chocolate chips

Cooking spray

> Did it take you as long as it took me to realize that coffee cake was not a cake with coffee in it, but rather something to be served with coffee? As a kid, of course, I thought the former, so when I was served coffee cake, it made me feel like I was getting away with something. I hope my kids are as confused as I was.
>
> —Howie

Note: This recipe makes enough for two coffee cakes. It's such a hit that one cake is never enough.

To make the crumb topping, in a medium-size mixing bowl, mash all ingredients together with clean fingertips until they are well mixed and crumbs form. Place the bowl in refrigerator while you make the cake batter.

Preheat the oven to 350°F. To make the batter, in a stand mixer bowl with the paddle attachment, beat the butter, sugar, and cream cheese on medium speed for 5 minutes, or until the batter is very light and fluffy. Add the eggs one at a time, mixing well after each egg is added to the batter.

Turn the speed to low and add half of the flour and all of the baking soda, baking powder, and salt. Mix until just incorporated. Add ⅛ cup milk and continue to mix on low. Add remaining 1 cup flour. Pour in milk and mix until batter is once again smooth. Add chocolate chips and mix briefly.

Spray cooking spray on the sides and bottom of the skillet. Pour half of the batter into the skillet and use a wooden spoon or spatula to smooth the top. Remove your crumb topping from the refrigerator and use clean fingertips to loosen the crumbs in the bowl. Gently sprinkle crumb topping over batter, making sure to get an even spread across the top, fully covering the batter.

Place the skillet in the oven on the center rack for 50–55 minutes, or until the topping is golden and a cake tester or toothpick comes out of the center clean.

Remove the cake from the oven and cool for at least 10 minutes. Serve directly from the skillet.

NUTTY BANANA BREAD

TOTAL TIME: 1 hour, 10 minutes

EQUIPMENT: 10-inch skillet

SERVES: 6–8

INGREDIENTS:

Batter:

2 bananas, very ripe/
　brown-black

1 tsp baking soda

1 tsp baking powder

2 Tbsp canola or vegetable oil

2 large egg whites

¼ cup brown sugar

½ cup sugar

¼ tsp salt

¼ tsp cinnamon

¾ cup white flour

½ cup whole wheat flour

½ cup sliced candied almonds
　(store-bought or use the
　recipe below)

Cooking spray

Candied Almonds:

½ cup sliced almonds

2 Tbsp sugar

¼ tsp vanilla extract

> I have no idea why "bananas" and "nuts" are metaphorically attached to going crazy. Why not refer to someone as "going mango" or "completely carrots"? My suspicion is that nutty banana bread is so good, going without it for any period of time disrupts our brain chemistry. But my suspicions are often wrong, so take that with a grain of salt. Speaking of which, why do we refer to skepticism as a "grain of salt?"
>
> —Greg

To make the candied almonds, if needed, add almonds, sugar, and vanilla to a clean, dry skillet. Place skillet over medium heat. After 2–3 minutes, the sugar will begin to melt into a syrup. Remove from heat and stir to combine. Spread candied nuts across parchment paper to cool.

Preheat the oven to 350°F. To make the batter, in a large mixing bowl, mash the bananas with a large spoon or fork, then stir in the baking soda, baking powder, oil, egg whites, both sugars, salt, and cinnamon until you have a smooth consistency. Stir in both flours and stir until just combined (no flour streaks). Mix in ¼ cup of the candied almonds.

Prepare your skillet by spraying with baking spray or spreading with vegetable shortening. Pour batter into skillet, topping with the remaining ¼ cup of candied almonds. Bake for 45–50 minutes, or until a cake tester or toothpick pierced into the center comes out clean.

Allow the bread to cool for at least 10 minutes, then cut and serve directly from the skillet.

SNACK TIME!

THE "I DON'T HAVE A PANINI PRESS" PANINO

TOTAL TIME: 15 minutes

EQUIPMENT: two 10–12-inch skillets

SERVES: 1 (feel free to multiply everything for a party or family)

INGREDIENTS:

1 soft ciabatta bread roll, split

4 slices fresh mozzarella, ¼-inch thick

5 thin slices ham

4 thin slices genoa salami

½ roasted red pepper, skin and core removed

1 handful arugula

2 tsp extra virgin olive oil

This one time I was in Italy and ate panini. A lot of panini. What's a guy to do? I walked into the panini shop and there they were, hundreds of them, stacked 4 feet high and 9 feet wide. Everything you think can go into a panini was represented. Through a cheesy and porky haze, I decided that the following panini is simple and the best of the lot.

—Howie

Pre-heat both skillets over medium-low heat on the stove for 5 minutes. Build the sandwich on the bottom of the roll in the following order for maximum everything-stays-together-ness: half of the mozzarella, all of the ham and all of the salami (fanned out), roasted red pepper, arugula, the remainder of the cheese, and the top of the roll.

Drizzle 1 teaspoon olive oil in the center of one of the skillets, and place the sandwich on top of the oil. Drizzle another teaspoon of oil on top of the sandwich and place the other pre-heated skillet on top of the sandwich to press it down evenly. Cook for 6–7 minutes, or until the sandwich is golden and crispy on the top and bottom. Cut in half and serve.

MONTE CRISTO SANDWICHES

TOTAL TIME: 35 minutes

EQUIPMENT: 12-inch skillet

SERVES: 6

Hold on a moment! French toast isn't just for breakfast? It's true. A little breakfast-time effort put into a lunchtime sandwich and you'll be happy to blur the lines between meals. My twist on a classic French *croque monsieur* heralds from my childhood full of Jewish delis and Italian grandmothers.

—Howie

INGREDIENTS:

4 eggs

1 cup milk

½ tsp salt

½ tsp garlic powder

½ tsp chili powder

12 slices (½ inch) white, rye, or
   sourdough bread

6 Tbsp mayonnaise

12 slices provolone cheese

1 lb corned beef, deli-sliced

6 Tbsp extra virgin olive oil

Preheat the oven to 200°F. In a mixing bowl, whisk together eggs, milk, salt, garlic powder, and chili powder. Pour this mixture into a rimmed baking pan, a 9-inch pie plate, or a wide, shallow bowl.

On half of the bread slices, spread ½ tablespoon of mayonnaise, one slice of provolone cheese, 3–4 slices of corned beef, another slice of provolone, and top with a second slice of bread spread with ½ tablespoon of mayonnaise.

Prepare a wire rack over a rimmed baking sheet next to the stove. Heat 2 tablespoons of the oil in a skillet over medium-low heat. Take the first two sandwiches and dip each side into the egg mixture for about 5 seconds.

When the oil begins to shimmer, place the first two sandwiches in the skillet. Cook each side until golden brown, 2–3 minutes. Remove the sandwich to the wire rack and repeat to finish all of the sandwiches, adding more oil to the pan, as necessary.

Place the wire rack and baking sheet in the oven for 10 minutes. Remove sandwiches from the oven, cut in half, and serve warm.

GRILL-LESS CHEESE

TOTAL TIME: 15 minutes

EQUIPMENT: 12-inch skillet

SERVES: 2

INGREDIENTS:

3 oz gouda cheese, shredded

3 oz block American cheese, shredded

4 slices (½ inch) white, whole wheat, or sourdough bread

2 Tbsp extra virgin olive oil

> I've never understood the "grilled" cheese sandwich. Sure, like any other red-blooded American kid, I've loved this delicious snack as an easy fix for years. But still, it bugs the living daylights out of me to call it "grilled." How often is it made in the yard over an open flame? I'm not changing the rules here, I'm simply changing the name. Who's with me?
>
> —Howie

In a mixing bowl, toss together the gouda and American cheese. On two of the bread slices, place a mound of half of the shredded cheese and spread it slightly, but make sure it does not go all the way to the edge of the bread. Top each with the other two slices of bread.

Drizzle 1 tablespoon of oil across the bottom of the skillet over medium-low heat. When the oil begins to shimmer, place the two sandwiches in the skillet and drizzle 1 tablespoon of the oil on top of the sandwiches. While the bottom cooks, gently press the top of the sandwiches with the back of a spatula to encourage the cheese to melt and spread further.

After about 3 minutes, slightly lift one edge and check the underside of the sandwiches. Once it is golden brown, gently flip the sandwiches. This may take more than one spatula or a daring couple of fingers on the top side to assure the sandwiches do not fall apart while flipping. After another 3 minutes, they should be golden brown on both sides.

Cut in half and serve hot.

QUESADILLA STACK

TOTAL TIME: 20 minutes

EQUIPMENT: 10-inch skillet

SERVES: 2–4

INGREDIENTS:

1 chicken breast half, about 5 oz, cooked and shredded

2 Tbsp salsa, hot or mild

1 Tbsp extra virgin olive oil

3 white or whole wheat 10-inch flour tortillas

6 oz Monterey jack cheese, shredded

2 oz can of diced green chiles

1 scallion, thinly sliced

Additional salsa, sour cream, guacamole, and cherry tomatoes, halved

> Quesadillas are a magical thing. They're fast, simple, and not altogether unhealthy. Perfect for a quick meal or late night snack attack, quesadillas are one of the finest Mexican imports after the sombrero! Typically, however, there is not enough variety in textures. Leveraging the skillet's ambient heat, these turn out crispy on the edge, chewy toward the middle, gooey in the center. Fiesta time, anytime.
>
> —Howie

Preheat the oven to 375°F. In a mixing bowl, toss the shredded chicken with the salsa.

Heat the olive oil in the skillet over medium heat. When the oil begins to shimmer, place one tortilla in the skillet. Top the tortilla with ¼ of the cheese, being sure to leave about ½ inch of the edge uncovered by toppings. Top the cheese with half of the chicken mixture, half of the green chiles, half of the scallion slices, and ¼ of the cheese.

Top this with one more tortilla, flatten slightly with a clean hand, and repeat the stacking of ingredients, starting with ¼ of the cheese. Again, be sure that the toppings do not spread all the way to the edge of the tortilla.

Top with the last tortilla and drizzle with 1 tablespoon of the olive oil. Place the skillet in the oven and roast for 15–20 minutes, until the cheese is melted and the top is golden brown and slightly crispy. Serve hot.

Cut the stack into wedges and serve with toppings like sour cream, guacamole, salsa, and fresh cherry tomatoes.

CRISPY TROPICAL FISH TACOS

TOTAL TIME: 1 hour

EQUIPMENT: 12-inch skillet

SERVES: 4-6

INGREDIENTS:

Taco:

1½ lb firm white fish (tilapia, snapper, cod, etc.) fillets, sliced into thin strips

2 limes, juiced

2 Tbsp extra virgin olive oil

½ tsp chili powder

½ tsp cumin

½ tsp salt

12 corn tortillas

2 cups canola or vegetable oil

2 cups lettuce, shredded

Salsa:

1 mango, diced small

2 Tbsp red onion, minced

½ red bell pepper, diced small

2 Tbsp cilantro, roughly chopped

¼ tsp salt

½ jalapeno, minced (optional)

1 lime, juiced

> Biting into a store-bought crispy taco shell is like swimming in a 95-degree pool on a hot day. It reminds you of something that should be pleasant, but is actually not all that great. Frying your own fresh tacos is a bit of extra work, but with the first bite, you'll know that it's worth every minute.
>
> —Greg

Whisk together a marinade by combining lime juice, olive oil, chili powder, cumin, and salt. Coat the fish in the marinade and store in the refrigerator for 30 minutes

While fish is marinating, prepare the salsa by combining all ingredients in a bowl. Cover and let sit at room temperature for at least 15 minutes.

Layer the tortillas on a large microwavable plate. Cover them completely with a damp paper towel and microwave on high for 45 seconds. Remove the fish from the refrigerator, discard the marinade, and place the fish on a paper towel lined plate.

Preheat the oven to 200°F. Place a rimmed baking sheet topped with a wire rack in the oven. As each taco is fried, carefully transfer the taco to the wire rack.

Heat the canola or vegetable oil in the skillet over medium. When the oil begins to shimmer, it is time to start frying the tacos.

Remove a single tortilla from under the damp paper towel. Fold the tortilla in half around a few fish strips and use a pair of tongs to pinch the top, where the two halves meet. Lower the folded portion of the tortilla into the hot oil and fry for 15 seconds, or until it holds a firm shape. Then, gently lower the taco into the oil, resting on one side. Fry until crispy and lightly browned, 60–90 seconds. Flip the taco and fry for an additional 60 seconds. Remove to the wire rack in the oven. Repeat until all tortillas are fried. You should be able to do 2–3 at a time.

Remove the tacos from the oven, tuck some fresh salsa and shredded lettuce into each and serve warm.

SUPREME JAPANESE PANCAKES

TOTAL TIME: 25 minutes

EQUIPMENT: 10-inch skillet, with lid

SERVES: 2–4

INGREDIENTS:

The Pancake:

1 cup all-purpose flour

¼ tsp sugar

½ tsp salt

¼ tsp baking powder

¾ cup chicken or vegetable broth, cooled; or water with 1 Tbsp soy sauce

4 large eggs

1 small green cabbage head, about 4 cups, cored and diced

½ lb shrimp, peeled, deveined, and diced

2 carrots, shredded

2 scallions, thinly sliced

½ cup panko breadcrumbs

> Japanese pancakes are also known as "Okonomiyaki" or "grill-whatever-you-like." What lies below is a cool approach to whatever-I-like. I like what I saw in Tokyo at an Okonomiyaki restaurant, where the tables have built-in griddles and they give you pancake batter and whatever-they-like. With any luck, you will like what I like, and if not, make these with what you like. Like?
> —Howie

1 Tbsp canola or vegetable oil

4 strips of bacon, halved

The Sauce #1 (Okonomi):

2 Tbsp ketchup

1 Tbsp soy sauce

1 Tbsp Worcestershire sauce

The Sauce #2 (Japanese-style mayonnaise):

2 Tbsp mayonnaise

2 tsp rice vinegar

¼ tsp garlic powder

In a large mixing bowl, whisk together flour, sugar, salt, and baking powder. In another mixing bowl, whisk together broth or water mixture with the eggs. Add the wet ingredients to the dry and blend until just combined. To this batter, add cabbage, shrimp, carrots, the white parts of the scallions, and breadcrumbs. Stir to combine evenly. Do not overmix.

Add the oil to the skillet over medium heat. Once the oil is shimmering, place half of the batter in the skillet and flatten with the back of a spatula. Then, with the front of the spatula, draw the edges back in to form a round pancake. Lay 3–4 strips of bacon across the top of the pancake.

Cover the skillet and cook for 6–7 minutes. Gently lift the edge of the pancake to see if the bottom is getting golden brown. Flip the pancake. Leave skillet uncovered and cook the other side for an additional 6–7 minutes. Repeat with the second half of the batter.

Drizzle both of the sauces across the top of the pancake, and top with the green parts of the scallions. Serve at room temperature or warmed, family style on a warm platter.

CRABBY RED PEPPER DIP

TOTAL TIME: 30 minutes

EQUIPMENT: 8-inch skillet

SERVES: 4–6

I moved from New York City to the Chesapeake region twelve years ago. Yes, I left real pizza and skyscrapers for love. Her alluring scent, beautiful eyes, and rosy glow drew this city boy away from Metropolis. I moved for the love of my life, my now wife. Or, was it the crab? No, it's definitely my wife. Did I mention the rosy glow?

—Howie

INGREDIENTS:

4 oz cream cheese, room temperature

¼ cup Greek yogurt

¼ cup mayonnaise

1 Tbsp lemon juice

1 tsp hot sauce

½ tsp salt

½ tsp smoked paprika

6 oz fresh lump crab meat

½ cup flat-leaf parsley, roughly chopped

1 scallion, thinly sliced

1 large red bell pepper, diced

2 Tbsp extra virgin olive oil

⅓ cup breadcrumbs

Preheat the oven to 400°F. In a large mixing bowl, add the cream cheese, yogurt, mayonnaise, lemon juice, hot sauce, salt, and paprika. Stir together completely. Add the crab meat, parsley, scallion, and all but 2 tablespoons of the bell pepper. Using a rubber spatula, gently fold these ingredients into the cream cheese mixture until they are fully incorporated.

Add 1 tablespoon of olive oil to the skillet and use a paper towel or a pastry brush to coat the bottom and sides of the skillet. Transfer the mixture from the mixing bowl to the skillet. In a small bowl, mix together the breadcrumbs and the remaining tablespoon of olive oil. Sprinkle this mixture on top of the skillet contents. Bake in the oven for 15–20 minutes, until the dip is bubbly and beginning to get golden brown on top.

Top with the remaining bell pepper and serve hot with toast, tortilla chips, or crackers.

SPICY QUESO FUNDIDO DIP

TOTAL TIME: 30 minutes

EQUIPMENT: 8-inch skillet

SERVES: 4–6

INGREDIENTS:

1 Tbsp extra virgin olive oil

4 oz raw chorizo, or other pork
sausage

1 tsp smoked paprika

1 tsp chipotle powder

¼ tsp salt

¼ tsp ground black pepper

1 Tbsp all-purpose flour

1 cup milk

5 oz sharp cheddar cheese,
shredded

One starry night, I had the rare opportunity to dine alone. With only one appetite to satisfy, I was feeling adventurous. So, I sat at the bar in a neighborhood Mexican joint. As I stepped through the door, the first thing that grabbed my nose was the aroma of smoky chiles and cheese! A steamy, molten skillet passed my schnoz en route to another patron. This was Queso Fundido! Here's my take on a restaurant classic.

—Howie

Preheat the oven to 425°F. Heat olive oil in the skillet over medium heat. When the oil begins to shimmer, add the sausage to the skillet and sauté, breaking it up with a wooden spoon until the sausage is no longer pink and beginning to brown, about 4–5 minutes. Add paprika, chipotle, salt, and pepper to the sausage and stir until you begin to smell the spices strongly, about 1 minute.

Sprinkle the flour across the sausage, mix it in thoroughly, and continue to sauté for another minute. Slowly pour in the milk while stirring it evenly into the sausage mixture. Bring it to a boil and set the heat to low and simmer for 2 minutes. Remove the skillet from the heat.

Stir in ¼ of the cheese until melted. Repeat until all the cheese is incorporated. Transfer the skillet to the oven for 5–7 minutes, until the dip is bubbly.

Serve hot with tortilla chips.

TOMATO AND CHILE POACHED EGGS

TOTAL TIME: 40 minutes

EQUIPMENT: 12-inch skillet

SERVES: 3–5

INGREDIENTS:

3 Tbsp olive oil

1 onion, thinly sliced

1 red pepper, thinly sliced

1 tsp salt

3 cloves garlic, pressed or
    thinly sliced.

1 tsp cumin

2 tsp paprika

¼ tsp cayenne (optional)

1 28-oz can of tomatoes, crushed

6 large eggs

1–2 Tbsp parsley, roughly chopped

> Growing up in Los Angeles, I thought that this dish was called Huevos Rancheros. Then, when I visited Israel, I found entire restaurants devoted to serving perfect shakshuka. Traveling through Italy, I found the same dish called Uova al Pomodoro. I'm not sure who the Johnny Tomatoseed was, spreading this dish as he traveled the earth, but I salute him. Here's to eggs poached in tomatoes! Long may it live!
>
> —Greg

Preheat oven to 400°F. Heat olive oil in a skillet over medium heat. When the oil begins to shimmer, add the onions, peppers, and salt. Gently sauté for 10–12 minutes, until peppers are soft and onions are light brown.

Move peppers to the outside of the skillet, leaving an open area in the middle. In that space, add garlic, cumin, paprika, and cayenne. Toast spices for 15–20 seconds, until fragrant. Then quickly stir to coat the onions and pepper with spices and allow to cook for 1 minute. Add the tomatoes. Simmer for 10 minutes, until tomatoes begin to break down. Remove skillet from heat.

Using the back of a spoon, create a small well in the tomato sauce. Gently crack an egg into this well. Repeat for each egg.

Place skillet in oven for 6–8 minutes, until whites are set but yolks are still runny.

Garnish with parsley and serve immediately with crusty toast.

HEAVY METAL PIZZA

TOTAL TIME: 60 minutes

EQUIPMENT: 10- or 12-inch skillet

SERVES: 2-3

INGREDIENTS:

1 recipe unbaked No-Knead Crusty Italian Bread dough from page 208

Flour and Cornmeal for dusting

½ cup Sunday Gravy from page 137 or canned tomatoes, pureed

3 oz pepperoni slices

½ red bell pepper, thinly sliced

4 oz whole milk mozzarella cheese, shredded

2 Tbsp Parmesan cheese, shredded or grated

1 tsp dried oregano

1 Tbsp extra virgin olive oil

> As a native New Yorker, I have an opinion about pizza. Go figure! Keep it simple! Pizza is about what you don't do to it. The finest pizzas in the world are brilliant in their scarcity . . . a suggestion of cured meat here, a smattering of green there, maybe a hint of a fresh vegetable for good measure. Be responsible in your art. Here I've suggested our family's favorite combination, pepperoni and bell peppers.
>
> —Howie

Preheat the oven to 450°F. Cut the dough in half. Place half of the dough in a plastic container in the refrigerator for later use. Roll the remaining half into a ball, dust with flour and cover with plastic wrap. Let the dough ball rest for 20 minutes.

Dust the counter or board with flour, place a dough ball on the flour, and dust the top of the dough with additional flour. Using a rolling pin, carefully roll the dough out to a 12-inch circle (for a thinner, crispier crust) or a 10-inch circle (for a thicker, fluffier crust).

Dust the 10- or 12-inch skillet with cornmeal. Transfer the dough circle to the skillet. Using a large spoon, spread a layer of tomato puree or gravy on top of the rolled dough. Top the tomato with layers of pepperoni, bell pepper, mozzarella, Parmesan, oregano, and drizzle with 1 tablespoon olive oil.

Place the skillet in the oven and bake for 20-25 minutes, until the top is beginning to brown. Remove the skillet from the oven, and transfer the pizza to a cutting board. Cut and serve.

CHEESY FRIES

TOTAL TIME: 45 minutes

EQUIPMENT: 10-inch skillet, 8-inch skillet

SERVES: 4

One evening when I was in college, I was dared to dip some French fries into a milkshake. It was actually delicious. I highly recommend it. If you don't happen to be near a milkshake, cheese dip is an excellent substitute.

—Howie

INGREDIENTS:

1½ lb russet potatoes, peeled and cut in ½ inch-thick sticks

6 cups canola or vegetable oil

1 tsp salt

12 oz bottle of light beer

½ tsp garlic powder

¼ tsp cayenne powder

¼ tsp salt

¼ tsp ground black pepper

16 oz Velveeta™ processed cheese, ½ inch cubes

Place potato sticks into the skillet as close to one layer as you can. Pour in oil to fully cover the potatoes by ½ inch or more. Turn the heat to medium and bring the oil to a bubbling boil. Cook without disturbing the potatoes for 20 minutes. Prepare a wire rack above a rimmed baking sheet next to the stove.

While the potatoes are frying, make the cheese dip by pouring the beer into another skillet and heating over medium-low. Stir in the garlic powder, cayenne, salt, and pepper. When the beer begins to simmer, add the processed cheese cubes. Stir occasionally until completely melted, about 8–10 minutes. Keep the dip warm for serving by turning down the stove to the lowest heat.

Once the potatoes have fried for 20 minutes, use a thin metal spatula, to gently ensure that the potatoes are not sticking to one another or the bottom of the skillet. Raise the heat up slightly, to medium-high. The oil will bubble more. Cook for 15 additional minutes or until the potatoes are golden brown. Turn off the heat and remove the fries from the skillet with a slotted spoon. Place them on the wire rack and sprinkle with salt.

Serve hot with cheese dip.

THE ONE-POT
CROWD PLEASER

CHEESE-LESS SPINACH LASAGNA

TOTAL TIME: 1 hour, 15 minutes

EQUIPMENT: 10-inch skillet, with lid

SERVES: 4

For some, the favorite dish of our annual Passover feast was the brisket. For others, it was my Mom's oddly midwestern raspberry "jello mold." But for me, the highlight has always been this dish—humble spinach whipped up with some moistened Matza. For this year-round version, I simply substituted lasagna noodles for my namesake cracker.

—Greg MATZA

INGREDIENTS:

2 tsp extra virgin olive oil

½ small onion, diced

1 stalk celery, sliced thinly

1 carrot, grated

1 clove garlic, minced

12 oz baby spinach

1 large egg, beaten

½ lb no-boil lasagna noodles

6 Tbsp tomato sauce

¼ cup breadcrumbs

Heat olive oil in a skillet over medium heat. When the oil begins to shimmer, add the onions and sauté 6–8 minutes, until translucent. Add the celery, carrot, and garlic and sauté another 2 minutes. Add spinach, stirring occasionally, until the spinach is completely wilted, about 4 minutes. Remove the vegetable mixture from the skillet and allow to cool for 5 minutes in a mixing bowl.

Once the vegetable mixture is cool enough not to cook the egg, add the egg to the mixture and stir to distribute it evenly.

In your skillet, spread 2 tablespoons of the tomato sauce over the bottom of the pan. Over that, add a layer the noodles, broken up to create a single layer. Then layer ⅓ of your vegetable mixture. Repeat two more times (sauce, noodles, vegetables), finishing with the vegetables on top. Cover tightly with lid or aluminum foil.

Preheat the oven to 350°F. While the oven heats, allow skillet to rest to begin hydrating the noodles.

Cook covered for 30 minutes. Remove from oven, uncover, and sprinkle breadcrumbs over the top. Return the uncovered skillet to oven for 12–15 minutes, or until top is lightly browned.

Allow to rest 5 minutes before slicing and serving.

FRACTURED LASAGNA

TOTAL TIME: 45 minutes

EQUIPMENT: 12-inch skillet, with lid

SERVES: 4–6

INGREDIENTS:

2 tsp extra virgin olive oil

1 small onion, peeled and diced

2 cloves garlic, roughly chopped

1 lb ground beef

1 tsp salt

½ tsp ground black pepper

1 Tbsp dried oregano

½ lb lasagna noodles, broken into bite-sized (2–3 inch) pieces

1 28-oz can of tomatoes, crushed or pureed

1 cup water

½ cup mozzarella cheese, shredded

½ cup Parmesan cheese, shredded or grated

1 cup ricotta cheese

> In my family, lasagna was something that only came from the frozen food aisle. I remember it taking hours to heat that enormous tin, usually resulting in overcooked, insipid noodles in a bath of fairly tasteless cheese. We submit, for your approval, a much faster, much tastier, much toothier animal—lasagna made on your stovetop in less than an hour!
>
> —Greg

Heat olive oil in a skillet over medium heat. When the oil begins to shimmer, add the onions and sauté 6–8 minutes, until translucent. Add the garlic and cook until fragrant, about 30 seconds. Add the ground beef, breaking it up with a spatula until no longer pink, about 5 minutes. Stir in salt, pepper, and oregano.

Place fractured noodles on top of the beef in one layer. Gently pour in the tomatoes and water. Bring to a light simmer, sprinkle the mozzarella cheese on top, then turn heat to low and cover with the lid or aluminum foil. Simmer until the pasta is cooked through, about 20 minutes. Add water if the pan becomes too dry.

Remove skillet from heat and remove the lid. Sprinkle on the Parmesan cheese and top with spoonfuls of the ricotta cheese.

If you want a brown, crusty top, place the lasagna 6 inches under the broiler until it reaches that classic lasagna color, about 3–4 minutes. Let stand for 5 minutes, and serve.

WEEKNIGHT PENNE

TOTAL TIME: 45 minutes

EQUIPMENT: 12-inch skillet

SERVES: 6-8

INGREDIENTS:

4 qt water

2 Tbsp salt

1 lb penne pasta

1 lb fresh green beans, ends
snapped off and halved

2 Tbsp extra virgin olive oil

1 lb bulk Italian pork sausage,
or links with casing removed

½ cup Parmesan cheese,
shredded or grated

½ cup breadcrumbs

> Don't get me wrong—I love tomato sauce. But sometimes I'm a bit burned out on pasta and tomatoes. If you, too, are on tomato overload, this quick, savory, cheesy dish is certainly the antidote.
>
> —Greg

Preheat oven to 375°F. In a large pot, bring water to a rolling boil over high heat. When the water begins to boil, add salt and pasta. Cook for 8 minutes, occasionally stirring to ensure the pasta does not stick to the pot. Add green beans to the pasta pot and continue to boil for 4 minutes.

While the pasta and beans are cooking, heat 1 tablespoon olive oil in a skillet over medium heat. Add the sausage, breaking it up with a wooden spoon into small bite size pieces. Sauté until the sausage begins to brown, but is still moist, 6-8 minutes. The sausage should finish at about the same time as the penne and green beans.

Using a slotted spoon, a spider, or a handled sieve, scoop pasta and beans and transfer into the skillet with the sausage. It's OK for some of the pasta water to come along for the ride, as it will help with the texture of the final dish.

Stir the pasta and beans into the sausage. Top the mixture with Parmesan cheese, breadcrumbs, and 1 tablespoon of the olive oil. Place in the oven for 12-15 minutes, or until the top begins to brown.

Serve hot.

BIG OLE SPAGHETTI PIE!

TOTAL TIME: 1 hour, 15 minutes

EQUIPMENT: 12-inch skillet

SERVES: 10–12

INGREDIENTS:

4 qt water

2 Tbsp, plus 2 tsp salt

1 lb dry spaghetti

6 large eggs

¾ cup light cream or half-and-half

⅓ cup, plus 1 Tbsp extra virgin olive oil

1⅓ cup Pecorino Romano or Parmesan cheese, grated

1½ tbsp dried oregano

2 cloves garlic, minced

2 tsp ground black pepper

1 large red bell pepper, roasted, peeled, cut into thin strips

½ lb baby spinach

My mother grew up with this dish and waxes nostalgic about seeing her grandmother's cast-iron skillet being brought out of the cupboard to make it! It filled her with anticipation of the chewy cheese and very top bits of crispy spaghetti. The first time I made it for my kids, those were their favorite parts, too!

—Howie

Preheat the oven to 400°F. In a large pot, bring water to a rolling boil over high heat. When the water begins to boil, add salt and pasta. Cook for 12 minutes, occasionally stirring to ensure the pasta does not stick to the pot.

Drain the pasta in a colander, spray with cold water to stop the pasta from cooking further and set aside while you prepare the other ingredients.

In a large mixing bowl, combine the eggs, cream, ⅓ cup of the olive oil, 1 cup of the cheese, oregano, garlic, 2 teaspoons each of salt and black pepper, and whisk until combined. To the bowl, add the spaghetti, spinach, and roasted pepper. Using two forks like salad tongs, toss the mixture together, evenly distributing the pasta with all the good bits of vegetable.

Add 1 tablespoon of olive oil to skillet to coat the bottom. Pour pasta mixture into the skillet and press the top with the back of a spoon to level the surface. Top the pasta mixture with the remaining ⅓ cup of cheese. Place the skillet in the oven for 25-30 minutes or until the top is just beginning to brown.

This dish is best served at room temperature, but serving it hot is still delicious. The cooler the "pie" gets, the easier it is to cut into beautiful wedges and serve with tomato sauce.

RIGATONI IN RED PEPPER SAUCE

TOTAL TIME: 1 hour, 10 minutes

EQUIPMENT: 12-inch skillet

SERVES: 6–8

I learned to cook from my childhood friend, Josh. Well, I say friend, but before he was my friend, he was that big neighborhood kid who taught me the joy of passing out from the pain of being put in a half nelson. On the other hand, years after reviving me, he did teach me to cook this amazing red pepper sauce. Thanks, Joshie!

—Greg

INGREDIENTS:

4 qt water

2 Tbsp plus 1 tsp salt

1 lb rigatoni pasta

2 onions, thinly sliced

3 red peppers, thinly sliced

2 tsp vegetable oil

3 cloves garlic, minced

1 14.5-oz can of chopped
tomatoes

½ tsp basil

½ tsp thyme

¼ tsp crushed red chiles (optional)

1 bay leaf

1 cup mozzarella cheese, shredded

⅓ cup Parmesan cheese, grated

Preheat the oven to 400°F. Heat the skillet over medium heat and add vegetable oil. When the oil begins to shimmer, layer the sliced onions on the bottom. Then spread the peppers on top of the onions. Let it lightly fry for about 10 minutes, until the onions are lightly browned and the peppers have begun to "sweat."

Add the garlic and stir everything together. Sauté until you can smell the garlic—about 30 seconds. Immediately pour in the can of tomatoes, including the juice. Add ½ cup of water along with the basil, thyme, bay leaf, 1 teaspoon of salt, and optionally, the crushed chiles. Turn the heat to low and simmer for 30 minutes.

While the sauce is simmering, bring water to a rolling boil in a large pot over high heat. When the water begins to boil, add the remaining 2 tablespoons of salt and the pasta. Cook for 10 minutes, occasionally stirring to ensure the pasta does not stick to the pot. Drain the pasta in a colander, and set aside while you finish the sauce.

Remove the bay leaf from the skillet and pour everything else into a blender or food processor. Blend the sauce until smooth.

In a small bowl, mix the mozzarella and Parmesan cheeses together. Pour the pasta, sauce, and all but ⅓ of the cheese mixture into the skillet, stirring to coat everything. Sprinkle the top with the reserved cheese, and transfer the skillet into the oven. Bake for 25–30 minutes, or until the cheese is nicely browned.

Allow the rigatoni to rest for 10 minutes before serving hot.

BAKED ZITI

TOTAL TIME: 1 hour

EQUIPMENT: 12-inch skillet

SERVES: 6–8

INGREDIENTS:

4 qt water

1 lb ziti pasta

2 Tbsp salt

2 tsp olive oil

1 medium onion, diced

½ lb bulk Italian pork sausage, or links with casing removed

2 cloves garlic, minced

1 28-oz can of tomatoes, pureed or hand-crushed

1 tsp dried oregano

½ tsp red pepper flakes (optional)

½ cup ricotta cheese

½ cup Parmesan cheese, shredded or grated

½ lb mozzarella, shredded or grated

Preheat oven to 400°F. In a large pot, bring water to a rolling boil over high heat. Add pasta and salt. Cook for 12 minutes, stirring occasionally to ensure the pasta does not stick to the pot.

Heat skillet over medium-high heat. Add olive oil. When oil begins to shimmer, add the onions and cook until lightly browned around the edges, about 4–6 minutes. Add sausage, breaking it up with a spatula into small bite-size chunks. Cook until the sausage browns, about 6–8 minutes. Add garlic and cook until fragrant, about 30 seconds.

Add tomatoes, oregano, and red pepper flakes, if using. Stir to combine. Bring to a boil and lower heat. Allow to simmer for 5 minutes, stirring occasionally.

Using a slotted spoon, a spider, or a handled sieve, scoop the pasta and transfer into the skillet, then stir to combine. Add the ricotta and Parmesan cheeses and stir. Sprinkle the mozzarella over the pasta.

Transfer the skillet into the oven and bake for 25–30 minutes, or until the cheese on top is golden brown. Allow the ziti to rest for 10 minutes before serving hot.

MEGA-TAMALE

TOTAL TIME: 1 hour

EQUIPMENT: 10-inch skillet

SERVES: 6–8

INGREDIENTS:

Filling:

1 Tbsp extra virgin olive oil

1 lb pork shoulder, ground

1 medium onion, diced

2 stalks celery, thinly sliced

1 tsp salt

1 tsp black pepper

½ tsp dry red pepper flakes

2 Tbsp all-purpose flour

1 clove garlic, minced

1 chipotle pepper in adobo sauce (canned), minced

1 4-oz can of diced green chiles (mild or hot)

1 28-oz can of diced tomatoes

1 14-oz can of black beans, drained

Growing up in an Hispanic neighborhood, I was invited to many a Christmas tamale party . . . family and friends boiling chicken, roasting carnitas, and the deceptively difficult stuffing and wrapping of the tamale. While nothing can quite replicate biting into that luxuriously steamed pillow of corn, this weeknight casserole does a very nice job of giving you the tastes of a tamale, without the hours of preparation.

—Greg

Topping:

1 cup yellow cornmeal

1 cup flour

⅓ cup sugar

½ tsp baking soda

1½ tsp baking powder

1½ tsp salt

1 cup buttermilk

¼ cup extra virgin olive oil

2 eggs, beaten

Preheat the oven to 400°F. Add oil and ground pork to the skillet and heat over medium heat. When the pork begins to sizzle, add the onion, celery, and spices. Sauté until the onions are starting to look clear, about 6–8 minutes. Sprinkle flour over the mixture, stir in, and continue to sauté until the flour is completely absorbed and you no longer see dry flour.

To the skillet, stir in garlic, chipotle, chiles, tomatoes, and black beans. Allow this mixture to simmer for 10 minutes until thickened.

While the chili is simmering, make the cornbread topping batter. In a large mixing bowl, whisk together cornmeal, flour, sugar, baking soda, baking powder, and salt. In a separate bowl, whisk together buttermilk, oil, and eggs. Add the egg mixture to the dry ingredients and stir until just combined but not completely smooth (no flour streaks). It's important not to overmix batter, as you want some small clumps throughout.

Carefully pour cornbread batter on top of chili in the skillet. Be careful that the batter sits on top of the chili and goes all the way to edges of the skillet. Place a baking sheet on the bottom rack of the oven, as the topping or the chili may overflow during baking. Place the skillet in the oven and bake for 30–35 minutes or until the cornbread topping begins to crack slightly.

Remove the mega-tamale from the oven and allow to cool for 15 minutes before serving in bowls with a dollop of sour cream.

LOBSTER POT PIE

TOTAL TIME: 1 hour, 45 minutes

EQUIPMENT: 8-inch skillet

SERVES: 3–4

INGREDIENTS:

Filling:

4 Tbsp butter

1½ cups water

½ cup dry sherry

12 oz lobster tails, shell-on and uncooked

1 Tbsp extra virgin olive oil

1 small onion, diced

2 celery stalks, thinly sliced

1 tsp salt

½ tsp ground black pepper

¼ cup all-purpose flour

1½ cups frozen peas

¼ cup flat-leaf parsley, roughly chopped

Crust:

1⅓ cups all-purpose flour

8 Tbsp unsalted butter, cold, cut into ½-inch cubes

½ tsp salt

4 Tbsp ice water

Flour for dusting

> Talk about old school! Pot pies haven't made a comeback like burgers, cupcakes, or fondue have . . . yet. It's high time for a pot pie revolution and it all begins on this page! I grew up on the frozen kind in that little tin, and couldn't wait to get to the flavor-soaked bottom crust. My version is quite grown up, and there's no bottom crust, but the level of silky decadence more than makes up for it.
>
> —Howie

Preheat the oven to 375°F. Heat the skillet over high heat and add the butter, water, and sherry. Bring the mixture to a boil and lower the heat to low. Maintain a simmer. Place the lobster tails in the skillet with the back of the shell down. Cook until the shell is just turning red and the meat is partially cooked, about 5–7 minutes. Remove the lobster from the skillet, and reserve the cooking liquid in a bowl.

Using kitchen shears, cut down the back and underside of the lobster tail, then carefully remove the meat in one piece. Cut the lobster meat into bite-size chunks and reserve.

Wipe the moisture out of the skillet and return it to medium heat. Add olive oil and when the oil begins to shimmer, add onions, celery, salt, and pepper. Sauté until the onions turn translucent,

Continued on next page.

about 6–8 minutes. Sprinkle the flour on top of the vegetables and stir to combine. Sauté for an additional 3 minutes.

Slowly pour your reserved lobster-cooking liquid into the skillet. Once it comes to boil, lower the heat and simmer for 5 minutes. Turn off the heat and stir in the lobster meat, peas, and parsley.

To make the pie crust, in the bowl of a food processor, with the regular blade attached, add the flour, butter, and salt. Pulse the mixture until a coarse meal begins to form, about 3–5 one-second pulses. Pour ice water into the bowl 1 tablespoon at a time, again using pulses, until you see clumps of moistened dough forming.

Remove the clumpy dough from the bowl, place on a work surface, and quickly work the dough into a smooth ball. Wrap the dough in plastic and refrigerate for at least a half hour.

Remove the dough from the refrigerator and place on a dusted counter or board. Dust the top of the ball with additional flour and use a rolling pin to form a 9-inch circle. It should be about ⅛-inch thick.

Place the dough round on top of the skillet and give it a moment to settle on the edges of the skillet. You can trim some of the overhanging dough, but leave some for dramatic effect (besides, people love extra crispy pie dough). Using the tip of a sharp knife, cut three 1-inch vents in the top of the pie dough.

Transfer the skillet to the oven and bake for 1 hour. Check that the top has become golden brown. If it has not, bake for an additional 5–10 minutes. Remove the skillet from the oven and let the pie rest for 15 minutes.

Serve hot in small bowls, or give spoons to some consenting adults and dig right into the skillet.

SHEPHERD'S PIE

TOTAL TIME: 60 minutes

EQUIPMENT: 10-inch skillet

SERVES: 4–6

I think that I would have been a pretty good shepherd. Spending my days leisurely strolling the grassy hillocks, idling under the shade of an oak, staring at my crooked stick, counting its rings, and wondering about the growth patterns of oak—while a wolf, three coyotes, and a band of sheep-thieves make off with half of my flock. On second thought, maybe I wouldn't have been that great of a shepherd.

—Greg

INGREDIENTS:

Topping:

2 lb russet potatoes, peeled, cut into 1-inch cubes

2 qt water

1 Tbsp plus ½ tsp salt

4 Tbsp butter, melted

½ cup milk

1 egg, beaten

½ tsp ground black pepper

Filling:

2 tsp extra virgin olive oil

1 medium onion, diced

2 medium carrots, peeled and cut into ½-inch rounds

1 cup mushrooms, chopped

1½ lb ground beef

1 tsp salt

2 Tbsp all-purpose flour

3 cloves garlic, minced

1 tsp paprika

1 tsp thyme leaves

½ tsp black pepper

1½ cups beef broth or stock

2 tsp Worcestershire sauce

¾ cup frozen peas

To prepare the crust, in a medium-sized pot, add the potatoes and water to cover. Add salt to the water. Bring to a boil over medium-high heat and then turn heat down to keep pot at a simmer. Cook until you can easily pierce a potato cube with a knife, about 8–10 minutes.

Drain potatoes, reserving them to a large bowl. Use either a potato masher or ricer to crush potatoes into an even consistency. Whisk butter and milk into potatoes. When the potatoes have cooled a bit, about 3 minutes, whisk in the egg and salt.

To prepare the filling, heat olive oil in a skillet over medium heat. When the oil begins to shimmer, add the onions and carrots and sauté 4–5 minutes, until the onions begin to brown. Add mushrooms, continuing to sauté for another 5–6 minutes, until mushrooms are tender and have released most of their moisture. Add ground beef and salt, breaking up the beef with a spatula. Cook until no longer pink, about 5 minutes.

Add flour and cook for 1 minute. Add garlic, paprika, thyme, and pepper and fry until fragrant, about 30 seconds. Add peas, beef broth, and Worcestershire sauce, and bring to a boil. Reduce heat to low and cook 10 minutes, until the broth has thickened to the consistency of gravy. Remove from heat.

To finish the pie, set oven rack to about 6 inches below broiler and preheat broiler to high. Gently spoon the mashed potatoes on top of the beef mixture. Using a rubber spatula or the back of a spoon, spread the potatoes evenly over the top. Place skillet under broiler for 5–7 minutes, or until potatoes are lightly browned.

Remove from the oven and allow the pie to rest for 10 minutes and serve.

CHESAPEAKE PAELLA

TOTAL TIME: 60 minutes

EQUIPMENT: 12-inch skillet

SERVES: 6–8

INGREDIENTS:

⅓ cup extra virgin olive oil

1 lb andouille or other smoked sausage, ½-inch rounds

1 large onion, diced

½ cup parsley, roughly chopped, divided

3 cloves garlic, minced

1 8-oz can of tomatoes, crushed

1 tsp salt

2 cups Arborio or other short-grain rice

4 cups chicken stock, broth or water

½ cup peas, frozen

1 big pinch saffron threads

12 oz shucked oysters

12 oz sea scallops, quartered

1 lemon, cut into wedges

> Paella has everything I love, all in one bite: rice, sausage, seafood, and veggies. What more could I ask for? Let me tell you. I could ask for a paella that uses the fresh seafood caught right in my backyard! This is a paella built for the Mid-Atlantic! But, still, it's kinda Spanish.
>
> —Howie

Heat the oil in the skillet over medium-high heat. When the oil begins to shimmer, add the sausage to the pan and sauté until the edges are browned, about 5 minutes. Remove the sausage using a slotted spoon and reserve in a small bowl.

Add onion to the skillet and sauté until the edges begin to brown, 4–5 minutes, then add ¼ cup of the parsley and the garlic and continue to sauté for an additional minute. Slowly pour the tomatoes into the skillet and mix them into the onions. Bring the tomatoes to a boil and allow them to reduce for 4 minutes.

Mix the rice into the skillet mixture and make sure that every grain gets coated. Pour in the chicken stock, broth or water, peas, and saffron. Add the sausage back to the skillet. Bring the mixture to a boil, then lower the heat and allow the mixture to simmer for 15–20 minutes, or until the rice is cooked through, but toothsome. Try a grain.

Tuck the oysters and scallops into the paella and simmer for an additional 5 minutes until the scallops are cooked through. To get a crisp layer of rice on the bottom, turn the heat up to high and cook for 1–2 minutes. When you smell toasty rice, you're done.

Top with lemon wedges and the remaining parsley. Serve in a bowl and suggest a squeeze of lemon.

CREOLE JAMBALAYA

TOTAL TIME: 1 hour

EQUIPMENT: 12-inch skillet, with lid

SERVES: 4–6

INGREDIENTS:

3 boneless, skinless chicken thighs, 1-inch dice

1 tsp smoked paprika

1 tsp salt

2 Tbsp olive oil

½ lb andouille or other smoked sausage, ¼-inch half moons

1 small onion, diced

1 green bell pepper, diced

3 stalks celery, diced

1 tsp ground cayenne or red pepper flakes

1 tsp ground cumin

1 tsp ground black pepper

1 clove garlic, minced

1 cup cherry tomatoes, halved

½ cup corn, frozen

1½ cups chicken stock or broth

1 tsp dried oregano

1 cup long grain rice

½ lb shrimp, peeled and deveined

> Jambalaya is my go-to dish, hands down. The beauty of this gem, aside from it being a one-pot-savior on a weeknight, is that you can add or delete veggies or spices to invent yet another new dish. My kids enjoy this with corn added, but let's start at the start, and enjoy the classic formula listed below! OK, fine, I'll add corn, alright, kids?
> —Howie

Preheat your oven to 375°F. In a bowl, season the chicken with ½ teaspoon of smoked paprika and ½ teaspoon of salt. Set the chicken aside.

Heat the skillet over medium heat and add the olive oil. When the oil begins to shimmer, add the smoked sausage to the skillet and sauté, stirring often until the edges of the sausage just start to brown, about 3–4 minutes. Add onion, bell pepper, celery, spices, and sauté with the sausage until the onion becomes almost translucent, about 6 more minutes.

Add in the garlic and sauté for one more minute. Add oregano, seasoned chicken, tomatoes, corn, and stock to the skillet and bring to a boil. Pour in the rice and stir to distribute throughout the skillet. Cover and move the skillet to the oven for 30 minutes.

Remove the skillet from the oven. Quickly tuck the shrimp into the jambalaya, and replace the cover. Allow the jambalaya to rest out of the oven for 15 minutes, or until shrimp is cooked through. Remove the lid, stir in the shrimp, and serve directly to bowls.

ARROZ CON POLLO

TOTAL TIME: 1 hour

EQUIPMENT: 12-inch skillet with lid

SERVES: 4–6

INGREDIENTS:

2 chicken breasts or 4 thighs, skin-on, bone-in

2 tsp salt

½ tsp ground black pepper

2 tsp vegetable oil

1 cup white rice

1 onion, diced

2 cloves garlic, minced

1 red bell pepper, diced

1 green bell pepper, diced

1 Tbsp tomato paste

1 tsp paprika

1 tsp chile powder

¼ tsp turmeric

1½ cups chicken stock or broth

10 green olives

½ cup frozen peas

¼ cup cilantro, roughly chopped

> Nothing makes me laugh like *I Love Lucy*. And nothing made Desi happier than his favorite dish—Arroz con Pollo. Sure, you could just call it chicken and rice, but who would ever want to? Babaloo!
>
> —Greg

Preheat oven to 375°F. Rub the chicken with ½ teaspoon each of salt and pepper. Heat 1 teaspoon oil in your skillet over medium-high heat until the oil shimmers, about 1 minute. Place the chicken in the skillet, skin side down, and let it fry for 3–4 minutes, until golden brown.

Turn the chicken, and continue to brown all sides, about 6–8 minutes total. Remove the chicken from the skillet. Add the rice into the skillet, tossing it and coating it with the rendered fat from the chicken. Stir for about 2 minutes until aromatic and very lightly brown. Remove the rice from the skillet.

Add 1 teaspoon of oil to the empty skillet and heat over medium heat until shimmering. Add onions and sauté for 6–8 minutes until translucent. Add the peppers, garlic, and the remaining 1½ teaspoons of salt. Gently sauté for 4–6 minutes. Add tomato paste, paprika, chile powder, and turmeric, and stir to coat the vegetables. Sauté another minute, until aromatic.

Add the rice back into the skillet, stirring until coated. Immediately pour in the chicken stock or broth and bring to a light simmer. Nestle the chicken into the top of the rice, cover, and place in the oven for 20 minutes.

Remove the skillet from the oven, add the olives and peas, re-cover, and return to the oven for an additional 10 minutes.

Top with cilantro and serve.

CUBAN CHICKEN THIGHS WITH CHICKPEAS

TOTAL TIME: 1 hour, 10 minutes

EQUIPMENT: 12-inch skillet

SERVES: 6–8

INGREDIENTS:

6-8 chicken thighs, skin-on, bone-in

1 tsp salt

1 tsp ground black pepper

1 tsp garlic powder

1 tsp cumin

1 Tbsp extra virgin olive oil

1 small onion, diced

1 red bell pepper, thin strips

3 cloves garlic, minced

3 Tbsp tomato paste

1 Tbsp soy sauce

2 Tbsp orange juice

½ cup chicken stock or water

2 15-oz cans of chickpeas or garbanzo beans, rinsed

2 tsp thyme leaves

2 tsp orange zest

1 large orange, cut into thin wedges

> Greg and I have this good buddy named Ray. He's Cuban. One day, Ray got hit on the head by a falling coconut. He absolutely loves this chicken dish. The delectable dark meat and crispy skin offer a strong counterpoint to the savory, creamy chickpeas. Anyway, Ray is doing fine.
>
> —Howie

Preheat oven to 400°F. Season both sides of the chicken thighs with salt, pepper, garlic powder, and cumin. Heat the oil in the skillet over medium-high heat. When the oil begins to shimmer, brown the chicken in the skillet, starting with the skin side down, about 4–5 minutes per side. Brown the chicken in two batches, so as not to overcrowd the pan. Remove browned chicken from the skillet and reserve on a plate.

Lower the heat to medium and add onion and bell pepper to the skillet. Sauté until the onions are translucent, about 6–8 minutes. Add garlic and tomato paste to the skillet and stir them into the onions and peppers. After about 1 minute, when the aroma of garlic is clear, add soy sauce, orange juice, stock or water, and chickpeas to the skillet and bring to a boil. Turn off the heat, and stir in thyme leaves and orange zest. Place the reserved chicken thighs onto the chickpeas, skin-side up, and transfer the skillet to the oven. Roast for 25–30 minutes, or until the liquid has reduced and the chicken skin has become crispy.

Squeeze a little fresh orange juice over the thighs and serve.

CHICKEN AND DUMPLINGS

TOTAL TIME: 1 hour, 30 minutes

EQUIPMENT: 12-inch skillet, with lid

SERVES: 8–10

INGREDIENTS:

Chicken:

1 4–5 lb chicken, cut into two legs with thigh, two breasts, and two wings

1 onion, diced

1 carrot, diced (about ¾ cup)

1 Tbsp dried oregano

4 Tbsp extra virgin olive oil

2 tsp salt

1 tsp ground black pepper

3–4 cups water

½ cup frozen peas

Dumplings:

3 cups flour

1 tsp salt

1½ tsp baking powder

2 large eggs, beaten

¾ cup plus 2 Tbsp water

1 stick butter, melted and slightly cooled

Place chicken, onion, carrot, oregano, olive oil, salt, and pepper in the skillet and turn the heat to medium. Pour enough water into the skillet to cover the chicken and come within ¼ inch of the rim. Bring the skillet to a boil and reduce the heat to low. Partially cover with the lid and simmer for 1 hour.

Turn the heat to low and transfer the chicken pieces from the skillet to a cutting board. Allow the chicken to cool while you make the dumplings.

In a large mixing bowl, whisk together the flour, salt, and baking powder. In another mixing bowl, whisk together the eggs and water. Continue whisking and slowly pour in the melted butter. Stir the egg mixture into the flour mixture until a dough forms. Dust the counter or a board and transfer the dough to this surface.

Using a rolling pin, roll the dough into a ½-inch rectangle. Using a biscuit cutter, cut rounds from the dough and set them aside.

Stir the peas into the broth in the skillet, place the dough rounds on top of the broth, and cover. Let simmer for 20 minutes or until the dumplings have puffed up a bit and the tops are cooked. Uncover and turn off the heat.

While the dumplings cook in the broth, pull the cooled chicken into bite size pieces and discard the carcass and bones.

Prepare a soup bowl with some pulled chicken, some of the broth and vegetables and, of course, a dumpling or two. Snuggle.

CALIFORNIA BLACK BEAN CHILI

TOTAL TIME: 45 minutes

EQUIPMENT: 10-inch skillet

SERVES: 4

INGREDIENTS:

2 tsp canola or vegetable oil

1 small onion, diced

½ tsp salt

½ green bell pepper, diced

½ jalapeno pepper, minced (optional)

4 cloves garlic, minced

1 tsp cumin

2 Tbsp chile powder

1 Tbsp paprika

½ cup water

12 oz canned black beans, drained and rinsed

1 medium zucchini, diced

¼ cup cilantro, roughly chopped

> I could write poems to the simple black bean. Small but powerful. Dusty in appearance, but exploding with flavor. But, as the skillet is more powerful than either the sword or the pen, I will make this dish my sonnet, my paean, my dinner.
>
> —Greg

Heat oil in the skillet over medium-high heat. When the oil begins to shimmer, add the onions and salt and sauté 6–8 minutes, until onions are translucent. Then add the peppers and garlic, continuing to sauté another 3–4 minutes, until the peppers begin to soften.

Turn the heat down to medium and clear a space of several inches in the middle of the skillet. Add the cumin, chili powder, and paprika directly onto the dry skillet. Stir lightly, toasting the spices until fragrant, about 30 seconds. Quickly stir spices into the vegetables and continue to sauté for another 30–60 seconds.

Pour the water into the skillet, then add the beans, and stir to combine. Allow it to come to a boil, then lower the heat to a simmer. Continue to cook, uncovered, for 15 minutes, adding water if the chili becomes too dry.

Add the zucchini and cook for another 6–8 minutes, until the zucchini is cooked through, but not mushy.

Served over corn chips or with rice. Optionally, you can jazz it up with sour cream and/or shredded cheese.

CENTER STAGE

ROAST CHICKEN WITH CARROTS AND GRAVY

TOTAL TIME: 1 hour, 45 minutes

EQUIPMENT: 12-inch skillet

SERVES: 4–6

Is there anything better than the aroma of a chicken roasting away in the oven? Forget your perfumes of sandalwood, patchouli, and bergamot. I want a gal who dabs the essence of freshly baked bread behind her ears. Roasted chicken on her wrists. Turkey stuffing in her hair. . . . Well, maybe I got carried away with the hair thing, but the rest sounds great, right?

—Greg

INGREDIENTS:

8 carrots, peeled

2 Tbsp extra virgin olive oil

1 4–5 lb chicken, whole

1 small onion, halved

1 lemon, halved

3 sprigs thyme

1 tsp ground black pepper

1 Tbsp plus ½ tsp salt

½ cup all-purpose flour

3 cups chicken broth, stock, or water

Preheat the oven to 425°F. Place the carrots in the skillet toss with ½ tablespoon olive oil, to coat.

Pat the chicken dry with paper towels. Into the cavity of the chicken, stuff the onion and lemon halves, as well as the sprigs of thyme. Use the skin around the chicken cavity to seal it shut. If there is not enough skin to seal the cavity, tie the ends of the legs together with kitchen twine.

Place the chicken atop the "raft" of carrots in the skillet, breast side up. Drizzle the remaining olive oil, then sprinkle the black pepper and 1 tablespoon of the salt over the chicken. Place the skillet in the oven and roast for 60–75 minutes or until the chicken skin is golden brown. Remove the skillet from the oven.

Using sturdy tongs, remove the chicken and carrots from the skillet and transfer to separate plates, reserving the juices in the skillet for the gravy. You may wish to tent the carrots with foil to keep them warm.

Place the skillet on the stove and turn the heat to medium. Sprinkle the flour and remaining ½ teaspoon of salt atop the pan drippings, and whisk them in until you no longer see white flour. Slowly pour the broth, stock, or water into the skillet and continue to whisk until there are no lumps. Bring the gravy to a boil and then lower the heat to low. Simmer the gravy for 5 minutes. If needed, add some water to get the desired gravy consistency. If the gravy is too thin, allow it to simmer until it has reduced to perfection.

Carve and serve the chicken with carrots and gravy on the side.

SOUTHERN FRIED CHICKEN FINGERS

TOTAL TIME: overnight brine, plus 30 minutes

EQUIPMENT: 8- or 10-inch skillet

SERVES: 4–6

INGREDIENTS:

2 cups sweet iced tea

1 Tbsp salt

2 lb boneless skinless chicken breasts

½ cup buttermilk

1 egg

1 cup all-purpose flour

1 tsp smoked paprika

1 tsp garlic powder

½ teaspoon salt

3–6 cups canola or vegetable oil

> There's this local restaurant chain I frequent in Northern Virginia where my kids consistently order the chicken fingers. They look delicious, so one day I took a bite (after asking permission, of course). It was a revelation. It was their tea brine! The meat was succulent, salty, and sweet instead of bland and dry. I thought, the only way to make these better is to take them all the way down south.
>
> —Howie

Add tea and salt to a large plastic container with a lid and stir until the salt dissolves. Cut the chicken breasts into ¾-inch "fingers." Place the chicken in the container with the tea solution, cover with the lid, and place in the refrigerator overnight.

In a shallow bowl or a pie plate, whisk together the buttermilk and egg. In a separate shallow bowl or pie plate, whisk together flour, paprika, garlic powder, and salt. Drain the chicken fingers and dry completely with paper towels.

Dredge the chicken, one piece at a time, in the flour mixture, shaking off any excess, then into the buttermilk mixture, allowing excess to drip off, then into the flour mixture once again. Place the coated chicken onto a plate and repeat with the remainder of the chicken.

Prepare a wire rack over a baking sheet and place next to the stove. Pour oil in the skillet until it's about 1 inch in depth. Heat the oil to 375°F over medium heat. If you do not have a thermometer, one handy trick is to use a wooden chopstick, like the kind you get with Chinese take out. As the oil heats, touch the tip of the chopstick to the bottom of the skillet at an angle. Once you see lots of bubbles forming around the entirety of the submerged chopstick, the oil is ready.

Carefully place a few chicken fingers at a time into the hot oil, being sure not to crowd the skillet. Flip each finger when the bottom becomes golden brown, about 2–3 minutes. After another 2–3 minutes, the chicken fingers are done and can be removed to the wire rack.

Serve hot with your favorite dipping sauce.

GINGER COCONUT CHICKEN

TOTAL TIME: 1 hour

EQUIPMENT: 12-inch skillet

SERVES: 4-6

> Ginger can be a potent flavor—even overwhelming. But a short braise in coconut milk mellows the flavor into a slightly spicy, luxurious Southeast Asian-style curry.
> —Greg

INGREDIENTS:

2 tsp canola or vegetable oil

2 shallots, thinly sliced

1 small red bell pepper, thinly sliced

3 cloves garlic, minced

½ cup ginger, peeled and cut into matchstick-size strips

1 pound chicken breast, boneless, skinless, sliced thinly

¼ tsp red pepper flakes (optional)

2 tsp brown sugar

1 tsp salt

½ cup water

8 mushrooms, stemmed and sliced thinly

1 carrot, ⅛ inch thin rounds

½ cup frozen peas

½ cup coconut milk

2 scallions, sliced thinly

Heat the oil in the skillet over medium heat. Add the shallots, red pepper, garlic, and half the ginger. Sauté for about 2 minutes, until the shallots begin to become translucent.

Add the chicken, red pepper flakes (if using), brown sugar, salt, and water to the skillet. Lower the heat to low. Stir the mixture until everything is well combined and allow to simmer for 8 minutes.

To the skillet, add the mushrooms, carrots, peas, coconut milk, and the remaining ginger. Continue to lightly simmer for another 10 minutes.

Stir in the scallions and remove from heat. Serve with white or brown rice.

ALMOND-CRUSTED PESTO CHICKEN

TOTAL TIME: 15 minutes

EQUIPMENT: 12-inch skillet

SERVES: 4

INGREDIENTS:

1 cup whole almonds, roasted and salted

1 cup all-purpose flour

1 large egg, beaten

1 Tbsp water

1 lb chicken breasts, boneless and skinless, cut into 4 even fillets

1 tsp salt

2 Tbsp olive oil

½ cup pesto, store-bought or prepared (see page 21).

Pesto is a fantastic summer sauce. And while the cheese and the basil get the limelight, I think that the key to a great pesto is a well-roasted nut. By doubling down on the nuts—having them both in the pesto and on the chicken—this dish celebrates the savory and salty aspects of pesto.

—Greg

Add almonds to a food processor and grind the almonds for 30 seconds, until they are the texture of breadcrumbs.

Using three shallow bowls, set up a dredging station. In the first bowl, place the flour. In the second bowl, whisk together the egg and water. In the third bowl, mix the almond crumbs with salt. Place a clean plate at the end of the dredging station. Dip one chicken strip into the flour and shake off excess. Then, dip the chicken into the egg mixture and let excess drip away. Then, dip it into the almond crumbs to coat and place on the plate. Repeat with the remainder of the chicken and set the plate aside.

Prepare a wire rack over a baking sheet and place next to the stove. Place skillet over medium-high heat. Add 1 tablespoon of olive oil. When the oil begins to shimmer, place chicken in the skillet and fry for 4 minutes, until lightly browned. Flip and fry the reverse side for 2 minutes. Remove to wire rack. Repeat for all the chicken, adding oil as necessary.

Serve chicken hot with a generous amount of pesto.

PORK CHOPS AND RED PEPPER RELISH

TOTAL TIME: 1 hour, 30 minutes

EQUIPMENT: 12-inch skillet

SERVES: 4

INGREDIENTS:

Chops:

4 bone-in center cut pork chops

2 tsp table salt

2 tsp sugar

4 tsp olive oil

2 tsp ground black pepper

Relish:

2 tsp extra virgin olive oil

1 onion, diced

1 tsp salt

2 red peppers, diced

½ tsp ground cayenne *(optional)*

½ cup tomato puree

As a middle child, I always identified with Peter Brady. And no more so than when he decided to emulate the great Humphrey Bogart with the memorable line, "pork chop'sh . . . and apple shaush." In his honor, I present this simple, updated take on the classic, where a totally different (yet still red) fruit is the star.

—Greg

Sprinkle salt and sugar over the pork chops. This can be done immediately before cooking, but for best results leave the salted and sugared chops, uncovered on the counter, for 1 hour, or in the refrigerator for between 1 hour and overnight. If you refrigerate the chops, be sure to remove them from the fridge 1 hour before cooking.

While the chops are resting, prepare the relish by heating olive oil in a skillet over medium heat. When the oil begins to shimmer, add the onion and salt and sauté for 4–6 minutes, until onions begin to become translucent. Add the red pepper and the cayenne, continuing to sauté another 6–8 minutes, until the peppers begin to lightly brown on the edges.

Add tomato puree to the skillet and stir through. Allow the mixture to simmer for 1–2 minutes until you reach the desired relish consistency. Remove from the skillet and allow to cool.

Preheat the oven to 400°F. Rinse and wipe out the skillet. Pat the chops dry with a paper towel, rub them with olive oil, and sprinkle with black pepper. Heat the skillet over high heat for

4–5 minutes. The skillet will be screaming hot, and you may wish to turn on the fans to full blast and open some windows. A good sear causes some smoke.

Carefully place each chop into the skillet and allow to sear, undisturbed, for 3–4 minutes, depending on the thickness. Flip the chops and transfer skillet to the oven and roast for 5–7 minutes. Remove the skillet from the oven, transfer the chops to a plate, and allow them to rest for 10 minutes under some aluminum foil.

Serve warm with the red pepper relish.

SIZZLING FAJITAS

TOTAL TIME: 30 minutes

EQUIPMENT: 12-inch skillet

SERVES: 4–6

Nothing benefits from cast iron more than fajitas. The non-stickiness, the superior browning, the heat retention, the ability to go stovetop to oven to table . . . all of these are leveraged in this simple, delicious crowd-pleaser.

—Greg

INGREDIENTS:

Marinade:

3 Tbsp extra virgin olive oil

1 lime, juiced

½ tsp garlic powder

2 tsp chile powder

½ tsp cumin

1 tsp sugar

1 tsp salt

¼ tsp cayenne pepper (optional)

1½ lb chicken breast fillets, boneless and skinless

Salsa:

4 tomatoes, deseeded, diced

¼ cup red or white onion, minced

1 jalapeno, minced (optional)

½ bunch cilantro, roughly chopped

1 tsp salt

2 limes, juiced

Main Event:

2 Tbsp canola or vegetable oil

2 yellow onions, cut into ¼-inch strips

1 green pepper, cut into ¼-inch strips

2 red peppers, cut into ¼-inch strips

3 Tbsp water

12 corn tortillas

In a mixing bowl, whisk together the marinade ingredients. Submerge the chicken completely in marinade. Allow chicken to marinate for 30–60 minutes.

In a separate mixing bowl, mix together all of the salsa ingredients. Allow the salsa to rest for at least 30 minutes.

Preheat the oven to 300°F.

Place skillet over the highest heat, Add 1 tablespoon oil. When oil just begins to smoke, add onion strips. Sauté until just charred, about 3 minutes. Remove the onions to a large bowl, and repeat with peppers in two batches, being careful to keep oil hot and not to crowd the pan.

Remove chicken from marinade. Add a splash of oil to the skillet, if it has gone dry. Add chicken to the skillet and allow it to develop a deep brown crust, about 5 minutes. Flip chicken and transfer the skillet to the oven until fully cooked, about 8–10 minutes.

Remove chicken from the oven and cut into ¼-inch strips. Place the skillet back over the highest heat and add 1 tablespoon of oil. When the oil begins to heavily smoke, add the sliced chicken, onions, and peppers back to the skillet and immediately bring the skillet to the table for serving. Sizzle and smoke. Just like a restaurant.

Serve with tortillas, salsa, and optionally, some sour cream.

VEAL MARSALA

TOTAL TIME: 35 minutes

EQUIPMENT: 10-inch skillet

SERVES: 4-6

INGREDIENTS:

1½ lb veal tenderloin, cut into
   8 3-oz steaks and pounded thin

½ cup all-purpose flour

½ tsp salt

½ tsp ground black pepper

2 Tbsp extra virgin olive oil

½ lb of cremini or shiitake
   mushrooms, stemmed and
   sliced thinly

½ cup sweet Marsala wine

1 cup chicken broth or stock

2 Tbsp butter, cold

3 Tbsp chopped parsley

Marsala is a fortified wine, grown in the volcanic soil of Western Sicily. Masala is an Indian spice blend, often featuring potent doses of cinnamon, cloves, and cardamom. Masada is a hilltop fort that overlooks the Dead Sea. Please do your best to keep these things straight.

—Greg

Mix flour with ¼ teaspoon each of salt and pepper. Lightly dredge the veal in flour, shaking off any excess.

Heat the skillet over medium heat. Add 1 tablespoon olive oil. When oil begins to shimmer, fry veal in small batches, until lightly browned, about 1 minute per side. As the veal is fried, reserve steaks on a plate.

Increase heat to medium-high, adding remaining olive oil. Add mushrooms to skillet and sauté for 6-8 minutes, until lightly browned. Pour Marsala wine into the skillet and use a spatula to scrape browned bits from the bottom. Cook until the wine comes to a full boil, about 1 minute, then add chicken broth or stock. Bring it to a boil, then turn the heat down to low and simmer.

Allow sauce to simmer for about 10 minutes, until it has reduced by half. Stir in butter and season sauce with remaining ¼ teaspoon each of salt and pepper.

Gently return the veal to the skillet, just long enough to heat the veal back to serving temperature, about 1-2 minutes. Serve veal with a generous amount of sauce.

BEEF BURGUNDY

TOTAL TIME: 2 hours, 10 minutes

EQUIPMENT: 12-inch skillet

SERVES: 4-6

INGREDIENTS

2 tsp extra virgin olive oil

3 strips bacon, diced into ¼-inch pieces

1½ lb beef chuck, fat trimmed, cut into 1-inch cubes

1 tsp salt

½ tsp ground black pepper

½ pound cremini or button mushrooms, stemmed and thinly sliced

2 carrots, sliced into 1-inch pieces

1 medium onion, diced

2 Tbsp all-purpose flour

2 cloves garlic, minced

1½ cups Pinot Noir or other light red

1 cup beef stock or broth

1 Tbsp tomato paste

½ tsp thyme leaves

2 Tbsp butter

¼ cup parsley, roughly chopped

Howie and I first met while working at a family camp. At this camp, I had the world's best job—hosting the late-night adult wine tasting. Over the course of three years, I was responsible for tasting (and often finishing) over 600 different bottles of wine. Nice work if you can get it, indeed! The smell of this dish, featuring my favorite varietal, transports me back to those late nights and early, headachy mornings.

—Greg

Preheat the oven to 300°F. Place the skillet over medium-high heat. Add oil. When oil begins to shimmer, add the bacon and cook for 6-8 minutes, or until it browns. Using a slotted spoon, remove bacon to a large bowl, keeping the fat in the skillet.

Season the beef with ½ teaspoon of salt and pepper. In three batches, add the beef to the skillet and brown on all sides, about 4-5 minutes per batch. Remove beef to the bowl with the bacon, again preserving the fat in the skillet.

Add the mushrooms, carrots, and onions, along with ½ teaspoon of salt to the skillet. Sauté for 8-12 minutes, or until the onions are translucent and lightly browned. Sprinkle flour on top of the vegetables and stir through. Add garlic and cook an additional 30 seconds. Once you can smell the garlic, pour in the wine, scraping the bottom of the skillet to release any browned bits.

Pour in the beef stock or broth, then stir in the tomato paste until dissolved. To the skillet, add the browned bacon and beef. If necessary, add a bit of water so that the beef is about ⅔ covered. Add thyme and cover the skillet. Place skillet in oven for 90 minutes.

Remove skillet from oven. Top with parsley and serve with No-Knead Crusty Italian Bread from page 208.

SHANGHAI RED RIBS

TOTAL TIME: 3 hours

EQUIPMENT: 12-inch skillet, plus a lid

SERVES: 4–6

INGREDIENTS:

4 scallions

2-inch piece of ginger, washed thoroughly and sliced into ¼-inch slices

4 garlic cloves, halved

3 pieces dried star anise

1 stick cinnamon

1 lb pork ribs, cut in half, crosswise (ask your butcher to do this)

⅓ cup Chinese rice wine or dry Sherry

2 Tbsp soy sauce

1 Tbsp molasses

3 Tbsp brown sugar

9 cups plus 1 Tbsp water

2 tsp cornstarch

1 bunch of broccoli, cut into florets

> I moved to China in 1996 and my first port of call was Shanghai. In honor of my first sight, smell, and taste of real Chinese cuisine, I present this dish as a representative of my adoration for China's delicious traditions. In fact, if you combine this with the first three recipes in "The Spread" (pages 161–165), it makes up one really fine authentic Chinese meal. Enjoy!
>
> —Howie

Cut the scallions in half, lengthwise. Place the whiter halves in the skillet. Thinly slice the greener halves and reserve in a small bowl. To the skillet, add the ginger, garlic, star anise, and cinnamon. Place the ribs on top of the vegetables and aromatics. Add rice wine or sherry, the soy sauce, molasses, sugar, and 3 cups of water to the skillet. Bring the skillet to boil.

Lower the heat to low and cover the skillet. Simmer for 1 hour. Uncover the skillet and continue to simmer for an additional hour. Using a slotted spoon, remove all solids. Discard everything but the ribs. If you want to, you can very easily remove the bones from the rib meat by hand. Return the ribs to the skillet over high heat. Mix together cornstarch and 1 tablespoon of water, and add this slurry to the skillet. The liquid will thicken. Lower the heat to low and simmer, uncovered for 20 minutes.

In a separate pot, boil the remaining 6 cups of water and add the broccoli florets, continuing to boil for an additional 4–5 minutes or until they are cooked to taste. Top the ribs with the reserved sliced scallion greens, and serve with broccoli and warm rice. For a balanced Chinese meal, serve alongside the first three dishes from next chapter.

BACON-WRAPPED STEAK

TOTAL TIME: 20 minutes

EQUIPMENT: 12-inch skillet

SERVES: 4

INGREDIENTS:

1½ tsp salt

1 tsp ground black pepper

4 beef fillets or other thickly cut steaks, 2 Inches thick

4 strips bacon

2 Tbsp butter

2 Tbsp extra virgin olive oil

4 rosemary sprigs

I was a child of the 70s. As a five-year-old, I had three different pairs of plaid pants in colors that would make a golfer cry. I think we're all happy that plaid pants, like Disco and Macrame, largely disappeared by 1984. But there is one piece of 70s cuisine that deserves a comeback: bacon-wrapping. I remember bacon-wrapped dates, bacon-wrapped water chestnuts, bacon-wrapped liver. This recipe is my attempt to bring back the tradition of bacon wrapping via its most luxurious incarnation, the bacon-wrapped fillet.

—Greg

Preheat the oven to 450°F. Generously season steaks with salt and pepper. Wrap bacon around the outside of the steak, securing it with a toothpick.

Heat the skillet over high heat. Add butter and olive oil. When butter is melted and beginning to bubble, add steaks to the skillet and sear until well browned, about 1–1½ minutes. Flip steaks and repeat on opposite side.

Top the steaks with a sprig of rosemary each and move skillet to the oven. For medium rare, cook for 7–8 minutes.

Remove from heat and allow to rest for at least 5 minutes before serving.

CHOPPED PORK AND RED SLAW SANDWICHES

TOTAL TIME: 6 hours and 35 minutes

EQUIPMENT: 8- to 10-inch skillet

SERVES: 8–10

INGREDIENTS:

Pork:

3 lb boneless pork shoulder or Boston butt (in one piece)

2 Tbsp salt

1 Tbsp sugar

2 Tbsp smoked paprika

Slaw:

1/3 cup red wine vinegar

1 lime, juiced

2 Tbsp sugar

1 tsp salt

½ tsp black pepper, ground

1/3 cup extra virgin olive oil

½ head red cabbage, very thinly sliced

½ red onion, very thinly sliced

1 small red bell pepper, very thinly sliced

8–10 soft potato buns

1 tsp mayonnaise per roll

> Everyone around me has their go-to barbecue joint. Mine, in particular, is a grueling six-hour drive from my house, is only open seven months of the year, and they lock the door when they sell out each day! This does wonders for my waistline, but is rather cruel to my love for pulled pork. So, this simple recipe is my awesome solution for a horrible dilemma. Waistline be damned!
>
> —Howie

Preheat the oven to 250°F. Mix together salt, sugar, and paprika in a mixing bowl. Rub spice mixture over every surface of the pork. Place the pork into the skillet. Whatever spice mixture failed to stick to the pork, sprinkle on top of the pork. Ideally, your piece of pork has one side with solid fat. This side should be face up in the skillet. Roast the pork in the oven, uncovered, for 6 hours.

In a mixing bowl, whisk together vinegar, lime juice, sugar, salt, and pepper. Slowly drizzle in the olive oil while continuing to whisk, until the dressing is combined evenly. Mix the cabbage, onion, and bell pepper into the dressing. Let the slaw sit in the refrigerator for at least an hour, covered. When the pork is about to come out of the oven, remove slaw from the refrigerator and remix. Set aside.

Remove the skillet from the oven and allow it to rest for 20–30 minutes, uncovered. Chop the pork into smaller-than-bite-size bits. Serve on buns with mayonnaise and red slaw.

MEXICAN CARNITAS

TOTAL TIME: 2 hours

EQUIPMENT: 12-inch skillet, with lid

SERVES: 8–10

INGREDIENTS:

1½ Tbsp extra virgin olive oil

2 Tbsp salt

2 tsp cumin

2 tsp garlic powder

2 tsp chili powder

3–4 lb boneless pork shoulder or Boston butt, cut into 2-inch chunks

¼ cup water

> Traditionally, carnitas is prepared by boiling a huge pot of pork in a gallon of oil for the better part of a day. It's terrific, but the quantities involved (both in pork and time) make it tough for most home-cooks to pull off. Below is a recipe that allows you to re-create the tender, moist crispiness of great carnitas through oven roasting right in your skillet.
>
> —Greg

Heat the oven to 350°F. In a large mixing bowl, form a paste from olive oil, salt, cumin, garlic, and chili powders. Add the pork chunks to the bowl and coat the meat evenly with the paste. Add the coated meat chunks to the skillet in a single layer. Then add the water to the bottom of the skillet. Tightly cover the skillet and roast in the oven for 1 hour.

Remove the skillet from the oven and increase the temperature to 425°F. Uncover the skillet, flip the pork cubes, and transfer the skillet back to the oven. After 25 minutes, flip the chunks again and roast for an additional 15–25 minutes, or until an obvious crust begins to form on the surface of the pork.

Using two forks, finely shred the meat, leaving some charred pieces to taste. Serve with warm tortillas, salsa, avocado, and lime wedges.

MEDITERRANEAN BULGUR PIE

TOTAL TIME: 2 hours

EQUIPMENT: 10-inch skillet

SERVES: 4–6

INGREDIENTS:

Crust:

2 cups fine-grained bulgur
  (sometimes called #2 bulgur)

3 cups hot tap water

1 Tbsp salt

1 Tbsp canola or vegetable oil

½ cup breadcrumbs

½ cup all-purpose flour

1 Tbsp ground cumin

1 Tbsp paprika

1 Tbsp honey

Filling:

¼ cup pine nuts

3 tsp canola or vegetable oil

1 medium onion, diced

½ tsp salt

2 cloves garlic, minced

1 lb ground beef chuck

1 tsp ground cinnamon

½ tsp allspice

1 tsp paprika

¼ tsp ground black pepper

Kibbeh are the corn dogs of the Middle East—spiced ground beef, stuffed into a shell of bulgur wheat, and deep-fried until deep brown. They are mouthwateringly delicious, but making them requires a great deal of expertise and time. When I'm cooking, I prefer to make it in pie form—the same ingredients, the same taste, but with a whole lot less work.

—Greg

Preheat the oven to 350°F.

To prepare your crust, place bulgur and hot water into a large mixing bowl. Allow to soak for 20 minutes until water is fully absorbed. Using hands or a wooden spoon, knead the salt and 1 teaspoon of oil into the bulgur for about 2 minutes.

Add the breadcrumbs, flour, cumin, paprika, and honey to the bulgur and knead for an additional 5 minutes. Cover and set aside for at least 30 minutes.

To toast the pine nuts, place a dry skillet over medium heat. Add pine nuts. Cook for 3–5 minutes, occasionally stirring and keeping a very close eye on the nuts as they will go from raw to burned very quickly. Remove from skillet when pine nuts are lightly toasted and fragrant.

Continued on next page.

To prepare the filling, heat 1 teaspoon of oil in a skillet over medium-high heat. When the oil begins to shimmer, add the onions and sauté for 3–4 minutes, until they begin to brown at the edges. Add the garlic and cook until fragrant, about 30 seconds. Add the ground beef, breaking it up with a spatula until browned, about 6–8 minutes.

Move beef to the outside of the skillet, leaving an open area in the middle. In that space, add the cinnamon, allspice, paprika, and pepper. Toast spices for 15–20 seconds, until fragrant. Then quickly stir to coat the onions and beef, and sauté for 1 minute. Add the toasted pine nuts and remove the filling to a bowl.

Coat the bottom and sides of the skillet with 1 teaspoon of oil. Take half of the bulgur mixture and press into the bottom of the pan in one even layer. Spread beef mixture over the bottom crust and finish by spreading the last of the bulgur mixture evenly over the top.

Using a small knife, cut five decorative grooves into the top of the pie, first top to bottom, then side to side, resulting in several squares along the top.

Place skillet in oven and roast for 45–50 minutes, until crust is fully cooked and browned. Remove from oven.

Allow skillet to cool for 10 minutes and serve in wedges or squares.

ITALIAN FESTIVAL SAUSAGE AND PEPPERS

TOTAL TIME: 1 hour, 15 minutes

EQUIPMENT: 10-inch skillet

SERVES: 4–6

INGREDIENTS:

3 Tbsp extra virgin olive oil

1 red bell pepper, cut into ¼-inch strips

1 green bell pepper, cut into ¼-inch strips

1 large onion, cut into ¼-inch strips

½ tsp red pepper flakes

½ tsp salt

½ tsp ground black pepper

2 garlic cloves, minced

2 tsp dried oregano

4–6 links, about 1 lb mild Italian sausage

If you've ever been to a summertime street festival in New York City, two aromas spring to mind: powder-sugared funnel cakes and sausage and peppers. Big, long spirals of fennel-scented, glistening meat searing on a flat-top griddle . . . memories are made of this. You wait in a line around the block and finally they stuff a sausage into a soft bun and smother it with caramelized bell peppers and onions: the perfect stand-up meal. Now, your house can be that festival, without the lines or the folks walking into you while you eat!

—Howie

Heat oven to 375°F.

In the skillet, mix the bell peppers and onions with the olive oil, chiles, salt, and pepper. Make sure that the onion strips fall away from each other. Roast in the oven for 45 minutes or until the peppers begin to brown at the edges.

Remove the skillet from the oven and increase the temperature to 425°F. Add garlic and oregano to the skillet and stir them into the onions and peppers. Using the back of a spatula or spoon, create a uniform layer of onions and peppers at the bottom of the skillet and place the sausage links on top.

Using the tip of a sharp knife, pierce the sausage links two or three times. Return the skillet to the oven and roast for an additional 15–20 minutes, or until the sausages are browned. Remove the skillet from the oven and serve the sausages hot, on a soft bun, smothered in pepper and onions.

SUNDAY GRAVY

TOTAL TIME: 3 hours, 40 minutes

EQUIPMENT: 12-inch skillet, with lid

SERVES: 4–6

INGREDIENTS:

3 Tbsp extra virgin olive oil

8 oz pork, neck bones or spare ribs

3 mild Italian sausage links

12 oz pork shoulder or Boston butt, cut into 1-inch chunks

2 Tbsp tomato paste

2 cloves garlic, minced

1 cup red wine or water

1 28-oz can of tomatoes, pureed

2 tsp dried oregano

1 tsp sugar

1 tsp salt

½ tsp ground black pepper

> This is the stuff of legend. When I was a kid, on Sunday mornings we'd go to my grandmother's house, and upon walking in, I knew the gravy had already been on the stove for hours. A delicious cloud of deep aroma met us—slightly meaty, a tad sweet, and all kinds of savory. Then, grandma would playfully chase me out of the kitchen with a hot fork for getting all nosey!
>
> —Howie

Heat the oil in the skillet over medium-high heat. When the oil begins to shimmer, sauté the neck bones, sausage, and pork shoulder until they brown on all sides, about 6–8 minutes. Add tomato paste and garlic to the meat and stir to distribute. Slowly pour the red wine or water into the skillet, then add the tomato puree, oregano, sugar, salt, and pepper.

Bring this mixture to a boil, then lower the heat and simmer, covered, for 2 hours. Uncover and continue to simmer for an additional hour to 90 minutes until you get the thickness you seek.

Remove the meat from the gravy and serve on a separate plate. Mix the sauce into cooked pasta, or serve alongside fresh bread.

TOKYO KATSU CUTLETS

TOTAL TIME: ½ hour

EQUIPMENT: 10-inch skillet

SERVES: 4

INGREDIENTS:

Sauce:

3 Tbsp ketchup

1 Tbsp soy sauce

1 Tbsp Worcestershire sauce

½ tsp sriracha or other hot sauce (optional)

Cutlets:

4 6-oz pork cutlets,

1 tsp salt

½ cup all-purpose flour

1 egg, lightly beaten

1 Tbsp water

1 cup panko breadcrumbs

1–2 cups canola or vegetable oil

When traveling in Japan, I was surprised by the level of specialization in their restaurants. You want ramen noodles? Go to the ramen shop. You want soba noodles? Yeah, that's a different restaurant around the corner. This level of specialization allows a fanatical level of attention to detail, which you can taste in every bite. While I can't promise that your katsu will be as amazing as someone whose sole occupation is the production of fried pork cutlets, I can promise that it'll taste good. And if you want perfection, I'd recommend a quick trip over the Pacific.

—Greg

Whisk together all sauce ingredients in a small bowl and set aside.

Season each cutlet with about ¼ teaspoon of salt. Using three shallow bowls, set up a dredging station. In the first bowl, place the flour. In the second bowl, whisk together the egg and water. In the third bowl, place the breadcrumbs. Place a clean plate at the end of the dredging station. Dip one cutlet into the flour and shake off excess. Then, dip the pork into the egg mixture and let excess drip away. Then, dip it into the breadcrumbs to coat well and place on the plate. Repeat with the remainder of the cutlets and set the plate aside.

Pour enough oil in the skillet to about ½-inch in depth. Heat the oil to 360°F over medium heat. If you do not have a thermometer, one handy trick is to use a wooden chopstick, like the kind you get with Chinese takeout. As the oil heats, touch the tip of the chopstick to the bottom of the skillet at an angle. Once you see bubbles forming around the entirety of the submerged chopstick, the oil is ready.

Prepare a wire rack over a baking sheet and place next to the stove. Carefully place a few cutlets into the hot oil at a time, being sure not to overcrowd the skillet. Flip each cutlet when the bottom has been fried to golden brown, about 3–4 minutes. After another 3–4 minutes, the cutlets are done and can be removed to the wire rack. Repeat with remaining cutlets.

Slice the cutlets, against the grain, into ½-inch slices. Serve with shredded lettuce or cabbage, the sauce, and hot rice.

BAYOU GUMBO MEETS CITY GUMBO

TOTAL TIME: 1 hour, 30 minutes

EQUIPMENT: 12-inch skillet

SERVES: 4–6

INGREDIENTS:

½ cup all-purpose flour

8 Tbsp butter

12 oz Andouille or other smoked sausage, ¼ inch rounds

1 large onion, diced

1 green bell pepper, diced

4 ribs celery, thinly sliced

1 tsp salt

1 tsp ground black pepper

1 tsp smoked paprika

1 Tbsp dried oregano

4 cloves garlic, minced

2 cups chicken broth, stock, or water

1 15-oz can diced tomatoes

12 oz chicken thighs, diced in ¾ inch pieces

12 oz shrimp, peeled and deveined

1 cup frozen okra slices

2 scallions, thinly sliced

This book is full of Cajun- and Creole-inspired dishes. If there ever were two truly native cuisines in the US, it's some permutation of these two. Their flavor profiles are similar, yet Cajun comes from the swamps of Louisiana and Creole comes from the city. Often a single dish offers both varieties. Gumbo is one of these dishes. The Cajuns use more poultry and fowl, where the Creoles use more seafood. My gumbo offers the best of both, ya' hear?

—Howie

Heat the skillet over medium-low heat. Add the butter to the skillet and melt completely, then gradually add the flour until it is fully incorporated. Stir regularly every 30 seconds for 7–10 minutes, or until the mixture is the color of milk chocolate.

Add the sausage, onion, bell pepper, celery, salt, pepper, and paprika to the skillet and mix it into the roux. Sauté until the onions are translucent, about 6–8 minutes. Add oregano and garlic and continue to sauté for an additional minute. Slowly pour in the broth, stock, or water and then the can of tomatoes.

Bring the skillet to a boil, then lower the heat to low. Add chicken to the skillet and mix in. Simmer, uncovered, for 1 hour, stirring occasionally. Add shrimp and okra to the gumbo and simmer for an additional 15 minutes.

Serve hot with rice and top with scallions.

RED BEANS AND RICE

TOTAL TIME: 3½–4 hours

EQUIPMENT: 12-inch skillet, with lid

SERVES: 6–8 as a main dish

INGREDIENTS:

3 Tbsp extra virgin olive oil

1 small white onion, diced

1 red bell pepper, diced

2 ribs of celery, thinly sliced

1 tsp black pepper

1 tsp smoked paprika

1 clove garlic, minced

1 large or 2 small smoked ham hocks

4 oz ham steak, diced

8 oz smoked sausage or Andouille, diced

4 cups water

2 cans red kidney beans

1½ tsp salt

1 Tbsp soy sauce

3 cups cooked white rice

2 scallions, thinly sliced

> For a kid from Brooklyn, I've spent an awful lot of time in the bayou. One day, outside of Lafayette, LA, I went on a swamp tour, replete with birds larger than the boat, bugs louder than the motor, and alligators who wanted to eat me before I could deep fry and eat them. Clearly, it was a pretty creepy experience. The one thought that got me back to shore in my right mind was the prospect of a luscious, smoky bowl of red beans and rice to wash away the creep. Note: no gators were harmed in the making of this dish. But, I would have!
>
> —Howie

Add the oil to the skillet and heat over medium. When the oil begins to shimmer, sauté the onion, bell pepper, celery, pepper, paprika, and garlic until the onions are translucent, about 6 minutes. Add the neck bones, ham, sausage, and water to the skillet and bring to a boil. Stir to distribute the skillet contents evenly.

Reduce the heat to low and simmer, covered, for an hour. Rinse the beans in a colander with cold water. Remove the cover from the skillet, and add the beans, salt, and soy sauce. Simmer, uncovered, for an additional 2 hours, stirring the mixture occasionally. If it gets too dry, add water a ½ cup at a time. The final texture should be creamy. Serve in a bowl with a scoop of rice and a sprinkle of scallions.

BRAZILIAN FEIJOADA STEW

TOTAL TIME: 3½–4 hours

EQUIPMENT: 12-inch skillet, with lid

SERVES: 6–8

The brilliance of feijoada is the pairing of the rich, meaty, complex stew with the sweet freshness of simply cooked greens. We've chosen spinach for the recipe because it's easy to come by and easy to cook. But any green will do—from kale to collards.

—Greg

INGREDIENTS:

3 Tbsp extra virgin olive oil

8 oz slab bacon, diced

1 large white onion, diced

1 bunch parsley, roughly chopped

2 tsp black pepper

3 cloves garlic, minced

12 oz pork shoulder, 2-inch chunks

10 oz beef short rib, 2-inch chunks

10 oz raw Mexican or Spanish chorizo sausage links

4 cups water

2 cans black beans

1 tsp salt

2 Tbsp soy sauce

3 cups cooked white rice

1 lb baby spinach, sautéed and salted

Add the oil to the skillet and heat over medium. When the oil begins to shimmer, sauté the bacon until it begins to brown, about 4 minutes. Add the onion, parsley, and black pepper and sauté until the onions are translucent, about 6 minutes. Add the pork, beef, sausage, garlic, and water to the skillet and bring to a boil. Stir to distribute the skillet contents evenly.

Lower the heat to low and simmer, covered, for an hour. Rinse the beans in a colander with cold water. Remove the cover, add beans, salt, and soy sauce to the skillet, and simmer uncovered for an additional 2 hours. Stir the mixture occasionally. If it gets too dry, add water a ½ cup at a time. The final texture should be creamy.

Remove the meat from the beans and serve separately. Plate beans with warm white rice, spinach, and some of the meat.

PICADILLO NEGRO

TOTAL TIME: 1 hour

EQUIPMENT: 12-inch skillet

SERVES: 6

INGREDIENTS:

1 Tbsp olive oil

2 onions, diced

1 red bell pepper, diced

1 tsp salt

4 cloves garlic, minced

1½ lb beef chuck, ground

1 Tbsp ground cinnamon

1 Tbsp paprika

2 tsp cumin

½ tsp ground black pepper

4 tomatoes, diced

2 Tbsp red wine vinegar

½ cup water

½ cup raisins

²/₃ cup black olives

½ cup cilantro, roughly chopped

1 lime, cut into wedges

> This Cuban-inspired Picadillo makes for a great weeknight stew. Because we're starting with ground beef, it only takes an hour to make. But you'd never know that from the complex and intricate taste— the sweetness of the raisins complemented by the cinnamon, cumin, and tomatoes. My mouth is watering just thinking about it.
>
> —Greg

Heat skillet over medium-high heat. Add oil. When oil begins to shimmer, add onions, red pepper, and salt. Cook 6–8 minutes, or until the onions are translucent. Add the garlic and cook until fragrant, about 30 seconds. Add the ground beef, breaking it up with a spatula until no longer pink, about 5 minutes.

Add cinnamon, paprika, cumin, and black pepper, stirring to coat the meat. Sauté spiced meat until strongly fragrant, 30–60 seconds. Add tomatoes, vinegar, and water. Bring to a boil, then lower heat to low. Simmer for 30 minutes.

Add raisins and olives and allow to simmer another 15 minutes. Serve with rice and top with cilantro and a squeeze of lime juice.

CRISPY SALMON

TOTAL TIME: 4 minutes

EQUIPMENT: 12-inch skillet

SERVES: 4

INGREDIENTS:

4 5–6 oz salmon fillets, skin on

1½ tsp salt

1 tsp ground black pepper

1 Tbsp extra virgin olive oil

1 lemon, cut into wedges

I love the sea and all of its riches, I've always been on the lookout for the perfect way to cook fish and seafood. Not recipes, per se, but the ideal techniques. Can the modest cast-iron skillet be the answer I've been seeking? Crispy skinned, yet rare salmon, well-crusted yet silky cod (page 151), and scallops like buttah (page 153)! You decide . . . and you're welcome, in advance!

—Howie

Season both sides of the fillets with salt and pepper. Heat olive oil in the skillet over medium-high heat until the oil begins to smoke slightly. Add the fillets to the skillet, skin-side down and let them sear without moving for 3 minutes. Flip the fillets and sear the skinless side for 30 seconds then remove the fillets to serve. Done. Squirt the fillets with lemon juice and eat. I like mine with rice and greens.

BLACKENED COD

TOTAL TIME: 8 minutes

EQUIPMENT: 12-inch skillet

SERVES: 4

INGREDIENTS:

4 6–8 oz cod fillets

1 tsp each of salt, ground black
  pepper, chile powder, smoked
  paprika, garlic powder,
  cayenne powder, and oregano

1 Tbsp extra virgin olive oil

1 lemon, cut into wedges

In a small bowl, mix the spices together. Season both sides of the fillets generously with this mixture. Heat olive oil in the skillet over medium-high heat until the oil begins to smoke slightly. Add the fillets to the skillet and let it sear without moving for 3–4 minutes, depending on the thickness. Flip the fillets and sear the other side for 3 minutes, then remove the fillets to serve. Done. Squirt the fillets with lemon juice and eat. Once again, I like mine with rice and greens.

CHILE-BUTTER-BATHED SCALLOPS

TOTAL TIME: 6 minutes

EQUIPMENT: 8-inch skillet

SERVES: 2–4

INGREDIENTS:

8–10 sea scallops, abductor
    muscle removed

1 stick (½ cup) butter

1 cup water

1 tsp salt

2 tsp red chile flakes

1 lemon, cut into wedges

Heat the skillet over medium heat and place the butter, water, salt, and chile flakes in the skillet. Bring this mixture to a boil and add the scallops snugly to the skillet. Lower the heat to medium-low and maintain a simmer for 3–4 minutes to get a medium-rare to medium level of doneness. If the liquid does not reach the top of the scallops, scoop some liquid on top of the scallops throughout the cooking time. Remove the scallops from the liquid and serve with lemon wedges. You guessed it, I like mine with rice and greens.

FISH AND CHIPS

TOTAL TIME: 45 minutes

EQUIPMENT: 8-inch skillet

SERVES: 2–4

INGREDIENTS:

Fish:

1 12-oz bottle light beer

3 cups all-purpose flour, divided

2 tsp baking powder

½ tsp garlic powder

½ tsp ground black pepper

1 tsp salt

4 6-oz skinless cod fillets

3 cups canola or vegetable oil

1 lemon, sliced into thin rounds

During my first trip to London, I had one mission. Well, one mission apart from the classes I was paid to teach! That mission was to find the best fish and chips the city had to offer. It was a monumental goal, indeed. I ate a lot. I smiled a lot. Below is my rendition of my favorite find—a lightly crispy beer batter with hints of spice, courtesy of pepper and garlic.

—Howie

Chips: See the French fries part of the Cheesy Fries on page 69. In a separate skillet, start making these first, since they take longer! If you do not have two skillets, make the chips first, and keep them warm in a 200°F oven.

While you're waiting for the fries to fry, cook your fish. In a mixing bowl, combine beer, 2 cups flour, baking powder, garlic powder, pepper, and ½ teaspoon salt.

Pour oil in the skillet and heat it to 360°F over medium heat. If you do not have a thermometer, one handy trick is to use a wooden chopstick, like the kind you get with Chinese take-out. As the oil heats, touch the tip of the chopstick to the bottom of the skillet at an angle. Once you see bubbles forming around the entirety of the submerged chopstick, the oil is ready.

Prepare a wire rack over a baking sheet and place next to the stove. Place the remaining cup of flour in a shallow bowl. Dry the fillets with a paper towel. One at a time, dredge a fillet in the flour, shaking off any excess. Then dip the fillet into the beer batter and carefully lower it into the hot oil. Repeat with one more fillet. Don't overcrowd the skillet.

Fry the fish for 2 minutes, then gently turn the fish over and fry for another 2 minutes. Once the whole fillet is golden brown, remove it from the oil and place on the wire rack. Repeat the process for the remaining fish.

Serve immediately with slices of lemon for squeezing. I like mine with a dip of hot sauce mixed with mayonnaise!

LOUISIANA GLAZED SHRIMP

TOTAL TIME: 30 minutes

EQUIPMENT: 10-inch skillet

SERVES: 4–6

INGREDIENTS:

2 Tbsp extra virgin olive oil

1 medium onion, diced

3 cloves garlic, minced

1 tsp cumin

1 tsp red pepper flakes

1 tsp smoked paprika

1 tsp oregano

1 tsp salt

1 cup water

1 large lemon, juiced

2 Tbsp sugar, preferably brown sugar

1 Tbsp tomato paste

1 lb uncooked shrimp, peeled and deveined

2 scallions, thinly sliced

> If there's one dish that reminds me of my honeymoon food tour of the South, it's this one! That notorious heat of the Cajun glaze, coupled with the soothing sounds of New Orleans Jazz, created a memorable feeling second to none. If this dish brings you back to the first time you ever cooked it and who you were wooing, we've done our job!
>
> —Howie

Heat olive oil in a skillet over medium heat. Add the onion. Sauté, stirring occasionally, until the veggies start to brown at the edges, about 5 minutes.

Have a cup of water at the ready. Add garlic, cumin, red pepper flakes, paprika, and oregano and stir until you can start to smell the spices. Immediately pour the water into the skillet, preventing the spices from burning. Transfer mixture from the skillet to a blender. Add lemon juice, brown sugar, and tomato paste to the blender and puree.

Pour the puree back into your skillet. Over medium-low heat, bring it to a simmer, stirring occasionally, for 15 minutes, or until the sauce thickens to coat the back of a spoon.

Turn up the heat to medium. Add shrimp to the skillet and allow to simmer until the shrimp just begin to turn pink, about 3 minutes. Top with sliced scallion greens. Serve with hot rice.

THE SPREAD

SHENYANG TOMATO AND EGGS

TOTAL TIME: 10 minutes

EQUIPMENT: 10-inch skillet

SERVES: 4–6

INGREDIENTS:

8 large eggs

½ tsp salt

2 Tbsp canola or vegetable oil

3 tomatoes, cut into wedges

1 Tbsp soy sauce

1 Tbsp ketchup

3 Tbsp cilantro, roughly chopped or 3 Tbsp scallion greens, thinly sliced

I moved to a town outside of Shenyang, China in the late nineties and I fell in love with the cuisine. During one of my first meals there I was served a common home-style dish that none of the locals fawned over, but I was astounded. Is that scrambled eggs? With tomatoes? I still scratch my head when I try to figure out why this few-ingredient bit of magic is not on every Chinese menu in the states. It should be.

—Howie

Note about eggs and cast iron: If your skillet is seasoned, oiled, and hot enough, eggs will not stick to the sides or bottom. But, if they do, scrape out the skillet and keep moving forward!

In a mixing bowl, beat the eggs with salt until the mixture is of uniform color. Heat the skillet over medium-high heat for 3 minutes and add 1 tablespoon of oil. When the oil begins to smoke, pour the eggs into the skillet and quickly scramble them, but do not allow them to cook completely. The eggs should be in the skillet no longer than 1 minute.

Remove the eggs from the skillet into the original mixing bowl. Wipe the skillet out, and scrape any egg bits off of the bottom and sides.

Return the skillet to stove over medium heat. Add 1 tablespoon of oil to the skillet. When the oil begins to shimmer, add the tomato to the skillet and sauté until the tomato begins to release some of its liquid, about 2–3 minutes, then add the soy sauce and ketchup and allow them to simmer with the tomatoes for an additional 2–3 minutes.

Transfer the scrambled eggs back into the skillet and stir them into the tomato mixture, breaking up the curds into large, bite-size pieces with the spoon or spatula.

Garnish with cilantro and serve hot with rice.

BEIJING IRON SKILLET EGGPLANT

TOTAL TIME: 40 minutes

EQUIPMENT: 10-inch skillet, with lid

SERVES: 6–8

INGREDIENTS:

1 large eggplant, cut into ½-inch rounds

4 tsp cornstarch

1–2 cups plus 2 Tbsp canola or vegetable oil

2 Tbsp Shaoxing rice wine or dry sherry

¾ cup chicken broth, stock, or water

2 tsp sugar

2 Tbsp soy sauce

2 Tbsp oyster sauce

1 tsp red pepper flakes

8 oz ground pork

2 scallions, thinly sliced

2 cloves garlic, minced

> This one time in Beijing, I attended a lunch and the dishes were all pre-ordered. I love a good mystery. It was a "Peking" duck joint and I knew it was possible to see my favorite side dish come out of the kitchen. The fates were with me that day, my friends. To the table came a mysterious, screaming hot skillet shrouded by a lid. As the lid was mercifully removed, billows of steam dissipated to reveal creamy eggplant smothered in a bubbling cauldron of sweet and spicy pork sauce.
>
> —Howie

Preheat the oven to 425°F. Dust both sides of the eggplant rounds with 2 tsp of the cornstarch.

Pour oil in the skillet to about ½ inch in depth. Heat the oil to 360°F over medium heat. If you do not have a thermometer, one handy trick is to use a wooden chopstick, like the kind you get with Chinese take-out. As the oil heats, touch the tip of the chopstick to the bottom of the skillet at an angle. Once you see bubbles forming around the entirety of the submerged chopstick, the oil is ready.

Prepare a wire rack over a baking sheet and place next to the stove. Carefully place a few eggplant rounds into the hot oil at a time, being sure not to overcrowd the skillet. Flip each round when the bottom begins to brown, about 1½–2 minutes. After another 1½–2 minutes, the eggplant rounds are done and can be removed to the wire rack. Repeat until all of the eggplant slices are fried. Pour the oil into a steel bowl and set aside to cool before discarding and wipe out the skillet with a paper towel.

In a mixing bowl, whisk together broth, stock or water, sugar, 2 teaspoons cornstarch, soy sauce, oyster sauce, and red pepper flakes. Whisk until the sugar dissolves.

Heat the skillet over medium-high heat. Add 2 tablespoons of the oil to the skillet. When the oil begins to smoke slightly, add in the ground pork and sauté until the pork is no longer pink, about 2–3 minutes. Add $^2/_3$ of the scallions and all of the garlic to the skillet and continue to sauté until a strong garlic aroma emerges, about 1–2 minutes.

To the skillet, stir in the broth mixture and allow it to come to a boil. Turn off the heat.

Tuck the fried eggplant slices evenly into the skillet, assuring that each slice is covered with sauce. Spoon sauce over the eggplant, if necessary. Cover the skillet with a lid and transfer to the oven and roast for 25 minutes.

Serve immediately with hot rice. Let one of your lucky guests carefully remove the lid and be bathed in a cloud of Chinese bliss. Top with the remaining scallions and dig in.

SICHUAN FRIED RICE

TOTAL TIME: 10 minutes

EQUIPMENT: 12-inch skillet

SERVES: 4–6

INGREDIENTS.

2 Tbsp canola or vegetable oil

2 scallions, light part, finely minced, green part thinly sliced

2 cloves garlic, finely minced

3 large eggs, beaten

3 cups cooked white rice, cooled, ideally day-old and slightly dried out

½ tsp salt

½ tsp ground white pepper

½–1 tsp red pepper flakes (optional)

Before moving to China, my take-out order of fried rice included hunks of vegetables, cubes of red food-coloring mystery meat, and long swaths of scrambled eggs. It was a meal in itself. In China, however, fried rice is simply a meal filler, a slight departure from standard white rice. It's a humble starch made with the previous day's leftover white rice, the egg delicately coating each grain, the aromatics disappearing into the golden sea. Here, I recreate the genuine article. Note the lack of mystery meat.

—Howie

Heat the skillet over high heat and add the oil. When the oil begins to lightly smoke, add the white part of the scallions and quickly sauté until fragrant, about 30 seconds. Add garlic and quickly sauté until fragrant, about 30 seconds. Add the rice to the skillet. Slowly pour the egg on top of the rice. Be sure it's well distributed, covering the visible rice.

Stir the rice around to mix everything in the skillet. Every 30–45 seconds, stir the rice to mix it up again, but allow some of the rice on the bottom to stay put. This will create bits of slightly crispy rice in the end. After 3–5 minutes of cooking, the rice is done.

Top with sliced scallion greens and serve hot, alongside other Chinese side dishes, such as the Beijing Iron Skillet Eggplant from page 162, Shenyang Tomato and Eggs from page 161, and the Shanghai Red Ribs from page 123.

CLASSIC CREAMED SPINACH

TOTAL TIME: 10 minutes

EQUIPMENT: 12-inch skillet

SERVES: 4–6

INGREDIENTS:

3 Tbsp extra virgin olive oil

1 large onion, thinly sliced

3 cloves garlic, minced

2 lb baby spinach

¾ cup heavy cream

1 tsp salt

½ tsp ground black pepper

¼ cup Parmesan cheese, grated

The cow was first domesticated at least 10,000 years ago. But spinach doesn't show up until about 1,500 years ago. Imagine that! For 8,500 years steakhouses were stuck with empty ramekins, just waiting for this lovely side dish to arrive.

—Greg

Heat the skillet over medium heat. Add the onions and sauté until the onions become translucent, about 6–8 minutes. Add the garlic and stir through for an additional minute. Add a handful of spinach to the skillet at a time, allowing each handful to wilt as it is stirred through the onions and garlic.

Sauté the spinach for 3–4 minutes. Add the heavy cream, salt, pepper, and cheese to the skillet and stir the mixture until everything is evenly distributed. Turn the heat to low and allow the mixture to cook until the cream is thickened, about 6–8 minutes.

Serve the spinach hot.

LEMONY CAULIFLOWER WITH ARTICHOKES AND CAPERS

TOTAL TIME: 40 minutes

EQUIPMENT: 12-inch skillet

SERVES: 4–6

INGREDIENTS:

1 head cauliflower, cut into medium florets

1 Tbsp plus 1 tsp olive oil

¾ tsp salt

⅛ tsp pepper

1 clove garlic, minced

1 lemon, juiced

½ cup marinated artichoke hearts, diced

1 Tbsp capers, drained

Cauliflower shines when roasted at a high temperature. A simple roasting with salt and olive oil transforms this fairly pale, bland vegetable into a golden brown, sweet, slightly nutty treat. This dish accentuates that sweetness with meaty artichokes and the classic salty/sour duo of lemon and capers.

—Greg

Preheat oven to 425°F. Spread cauliflower florets across bottom of the skillet. Drizzle 1 tablespoon of olive oil over the cauliflower and sprinkle with salt and pepper.

Roast for approximately 30 minutes, uncovered, stirring lightly every 10 minutes to achieve even browning. Remove roasted cauliflower from the oven and transfer to a bowl.

Put the hot skillet over medium-low heat. Add 1 teaspoon of oil. When oil begins to shimmer, add garlic and fry until fragrant, about 20 seconds. Add lemon juice, artichokes, and capers, and cook for 1 minute.

Pour roasted cauliflower back into the skillet and stir to combine. Return to oven for a final 5 minutes.

Serve immediately or at room temperature.

GARLICKY ROASTED BROCCOLI AND CAULIFLOWER

TOTAL TIME: 10 minutes

EQUIPMENT: 12-inch skillet

SERVES: 6–8

INGREDIENTS:

5 Tbsp extra virgin olive oil

4 cloves garlic, minced

1 tsp salt

½ tsp ground black pepper

½ tsp garlic powder

½ tsp onion powder

3 cups broccoli florets

1 head of cauliflower, cut into small florets

1 lemon, cut into wedges

I used to believe that kids had a taste bud to specifically ward off broccoli and cauliflower, like it was an adult-only vegetable. "Some day, kid, you too will enjoy little trees like us big people." I was convinced, until I made this dish for my family. By the time I sat down at the dinner table, it would have taken tweezers to find what my kids left for me in the skillet. It's good to be a kid.

—Howie

Preheat the oven to 425°F. In a large mixing bowl, whisk together the oil, garlic, and spices. Toss the broccoli and cauliflower with the oil mixture so that the vegetables are evenly coated.

Pour coated vegetables into the skillet in an even layer. Place the skillet in the oven and roast for 15 minutes. Remove the skillet from the oven and carefully toss the vegetables with a spatula or wooden spoon. Return the skillet to the oven and continue to roast for an additional 10–15 minutes, until the edges of the broccoli and cauliflower begin to brown.

Remove from the oven and serve hot with lemon wedges.

UNION CITY EGGPLANT PARMESAN

TOTAL TIME: 1 hour, 30 minutes

EQUIPMENT: 10-inch skillet

SERVES: 4-6

INGREDIENTS:

1 cup all-purpose flour

2 eggs, lightly beaten

1 Tbsp water

1 cup breadcrumbs

1½ tsp salt

1 large globe eggplant, peeled and cut into ½-inch rounds

1-2 cups canola or vegetable oil

1 14-oz can of tomatoes, whole, crushed, or pureed—OR 2 cups Sunday Gravy from page 137

2 Tbsp extra virgin olive oil

½ tsp black pepper

1 tsp dried oregano

1 lb fresh mozzarella cheese, cut into ¼ inch slices

½ cup Parmesan cheese, shredded or grated

2 Tbsp basil, thinly sliced

> I once had a colleague who fed me this awesome German chocolate cake. It was delicious. But wait, where's that gooey coconut frosting? How is this a German chocolate cake? She said, "A friend from Germany taught me how to make it!" Sometimes, frame of reference outweighs origins. I learned how to make this dish from my little Italian grandmother in Union City, New Jersey.
>
> —Howie

Preheat the oven to 375°F. Using three shallow bowls, set up a dredging station. In the first bowl, place the flour. In the second bowl, whisk together the egg and water. In the third bowl, mix the breadcrumbs with 1 teaspoon of salt. Place a clean plate at the end of the dredging station. Dip one eggplant round into the flour and shake off excess. Then, dip the eggplant into the egg mixture and let excess drip away. Then, dip it into the breadcrumbs to coat and place on the plate. Repeat with the remainder of the eggplant and set the plate aside.

Pour oil in the skillet to about ½ inch in depth. Heat the oil to 375°F over medium heat. If you do not have a thermometer, one handy trick is to use a wooden chopstick, like the kind you get with Chinese take-out. As the oil heats, touch the tip of the chopstick to the bottom of the skillet at an angle. Once you see lots of bubbles forming around the entirety of the submerged chopstick, the oil is ready.

Prepare a wire rack over a baking sheet and place next to the stove. Carefully place a few coated eggplant rounds into the hot oil at a time, being sure not to overcrowd the skillet. Flip each

Continued on next page.

round when the bottom has been fried to golden brown, about 1½–2 minutes. After another 1½–2 minutes, the eggplant rounds are done and can be removed to the wire rack. Discard the oil and wipe out the skillet with a paper towel.

If you're using Sunday Gravy from page 137, skip this paragraph. In a blender or food processor, blend the tomatoes, olive oil, ½ teaspoon of salt, black pepper, and oregano until smooth.

Coat the bottom of the skillet with ½ cup of the tomato sauce. Form one layer of fried eggplant rounds on top of the tomato sauce. Spoon tomato sauce on top of each of the eggplant rounds, then top them with torn pieces of mozzarella slices, using about ⅓ of your mozzarella.

Form another layer of eggplant rounds on top of the first layer. Spoon tomato sauce on top of them. If you have additional eggplant rounds, form another layer of cheese, eggplant, and tomato sauce, but you're likely to have just two. So, spoon the remainder of the sauce over the whole top of the skillet, then top with the remainder of the mozzarella, and finally sprinkle the skillet with Parmesan cheese.

Roast in the oven for 45–60 minutes, or until the top is bubbly and dark brown in spots. Serve with pasta, on a sandwich, or just a fork and a smile.

SWEET AND SPICY SHAVED BRUSSELS SPROUTS

TOTAL TIME: 10 minutes

EQUIPMENT: 12-inch skillet

SERVES: 6–8

INGREDIENTS:

2 pieces bacon, diced

1½ lb Brussels Sprouts, stem removed, shaved thin with a mandolin or knife

1 red Jalapeno or Fresno chile, thinly sliced

OR 1 tsp red chile flakes

½ tsp salt

I hated Brussels Sprouts. When traveling in Europe I almost skipped the city of Brussels, simply because the word reminded me of that old-sock smell of steamed army-green globes. But shaved sprouts, I came to learn, were a different story. Cooking them in a hot skillet brings out a lovely nutty, peppery flavor. Add to that some bacon and chiles and you've got a dish that even a sprout-hater can love.

—Greg

Heat the skillet over medium-high heat. Add the bacon and sauté until browned but not crispy, about 3–4 minutes.

Add the chiles and stir them into the bacon, allowing them to flavor the oil for 30 seconds. Turn up the heat to your highest setting and add the sprouts. Sauté the sprouts, stirring them regularly for 3–4 minutes, until all are cooked through and some begin to brown.

Serve hot.

SWEET FRIED CABBAGE

TOTAL TIME: 35 minutes

EQUIPMENT: 12-inch skillet, with lid

SERVES: 6–8

4 pieces bacon, sliced into ⅛ inch strips

1 onion, cut into ⅛ inch strips

1 red bell pepper, cut into ¼ inch strips

1 head cabbage, shredded or very thinly sliced

⅓ cup chicken stock or broth

2 tsp apple cider vinegar

½ tsp sugar

½ tsp salt

¼ tsp ground black pepper

> Most people can't stand the smell of cabbage cooking away on a stove. I love it. I LOVE it. As a kid, whenever my mom was boiling cabbage, I would find excuses to hang out in the kitchen as everyone else hurried away. Maybe I just enjoyed the solitude?
>
> —Greg

Place bacon and in the skillet and heat over medium heat. Cook the bacon, stirring frequently until it starts to brown, about 3–4 minutes. Add onion and red pepper to the skillet and sauté until the onion starts to become translucent, about 6–8 minutes.

Turn heat up to high. One big handful at a time, add cabbage to the skillet and allow it to wilt slightly, mixed into the bacon, onions, and peppers. When all of the cabbage has been incorporated and wilted, after about 3 minutes, add in broth or stock, vinegar, sugar, salt, and pepper.

Stir to combine everything evenly, cover the skillet, lower the heat to low. Cook for 15–20 minutes, or until the cabbage is soft. Serve hot.

PERFECTLY ROASTED RED POTATOES

TOTAL TIME: 35 minutes

EQUIPMENT: 10-inch skillet, with lid

SERVES: 2–4

INGREDIENTS:

1 lb Red Bliss or other new red
    potatoes, washed and halved

7 Tbsp extra virgin olive oil

1 tsp salt

2 Tbsp water

I love potatoes in most formats, but when I began to experiment with little red potatoes, it was like a whole new world opened up. Imagine a world in which the crispiness of a French fry, the creaminess of mashers, and the toastiness of a baked tater all lived within a single bite. Imagine no more. You live in that world, now.

—Greg

Heat the skillet over medium heat and add 6 tablespoons of the olive oil. When the oil begins to shimmer, sprinkle the salt in an even layer across the bottom of the skillet. Place the potatoes in the skillet atop the salt with the cut side down. Allow the potatoes to fry for 9–10 minutes, or until the bottoms are a golden brown. It's OK if they need another minute or so.

Reduce the heat to low. Slowly add the water to one side of the skillet, watching for splattered or splashed hot oil. Drizzle the remaining olive oil on top of the potatoes and cover the skillet with the lid. Lower the heat to low and cook for an additional 25 minutes. The potatoes are perfect when you can easily slide a knife through from top to bottom.

Remove from the heat, uncover, and serve hot.

TOASTY, ROASTED SWEET POTATOES

TOTAL TIME: 40 minutes

EQUIPMENT: 12-inch skillet

SERVES: 4 as a side dish

INGREDIENTS:

2 lb sweet potatoes, peeled,
  ¼-inch rounds

¼ cup olive oil

½ tsp table salt

"Ugh, that's too sweet," I'd occasionally hear grownups say. "How can something possibly be too sweet?" I'd think to myself, while pouring maple syrup straight from the bottle into my gullet. Well, for better or worse, I've become one of those grownups for whom yams with marshmallows have become too sweet. So, I offer this simple preparation, which beautifully balances the natural moderate sweetness of the tuber with the earthiness contributed by high heat.

—Greg

Preheat oven to 450°F. Toss sliced sweet potatoes in olive oil and salt. Place the sweet potatoes across the bottom of the skillet. They won't all fit in one layer, but get as many laying flat as possible.

Place skillet in oven for 14–16 minutes, until sweet potatoes on the bottom begin to lightly brown. Remove skillet from the oven. Using a spatula, gently move sweet potatoes on the bottom to the side, allowing un-browned sweet potatoes to lie flat on the bottom. Return to oven for another 15 minutes, repeat the stirring, and return to the oven for an additional 5 minutes. Sweet potatoes should have a crispy, light brown exterior.

Serve hot.

MAPLE-SPIKED ACORN SQUASH

TOTAL TIME: 30 minutes

EQUIPMENT: 12-inch skillet

SERVES: 4

INGREDIENTS:

1 acorn squash

2 Tbsp butter

1 Tbsp maple syrup

¼ tsp salt

¼ tsp red chile flakes (optional)

This fall favorite is inspired by tempura, in that the skin is left on the squash. Not only does the skin look gorgeous, it keeps the squash slice in one piece and gives a crisp, satisfying bite.

—Greg

Wash the outside of the squash well and slice in half lengthwise (the knife should bisect from stem to blossom end). Clean out the seeds. Flipping the orange side down, cut the squash into about ¼ inch–thick slices, using the natural bumps on the outside to guide you.

Place skillet over medium heat. Add butter and cook until melted, 1–2 minutes. When it is just melted, stir in the maple syrup, the salt and, optionally, the chile flakes.

Reduce heat to medium-low. Add the sliced squash, frying for 6–7 minutes until light brown. Gently flip and cook opposite side another 6–7 min. Depending upon the size of the squash, you may need to do this in two batches. If the pan starts to dry out, just add a bit more butter and syrup.

Remove the squash to a serving plate, drizzle the pan sauce over the slices. Serve hot.

CORN CASSEROLE

TOTAL TIME: 55 minutes

EQUIPMENT: 10-inch skillet

SERVES: 6–8

INGREDIENTS:

1 cup yellow cornmeal

⅓ cup all-purpose flour

¼ cup sugar

¼ tsp baking soda

½ tsp baking powder

1 cup buttermilk

½ tsp salt

1 4-oz can diced green chilies

1 16-oz can creamed corn

2 large eggs, beaten

¼ cup plus 1 Tbsp extra virgin olive oil

½ cup sharp cheddar cheese, shredded

I'm one of those people who prefers eating raisins out of a box and not in a cookie. I feel the opposite way about corn. On the cob? Why would I ever do that? But, in a confusing dish that's not exactly a bread, not exactly a veggie side dish, and not exactly a pudding, I'm in my comfort zone. I'm a weirdo.

—Howie

Preheat the oven to 375°F. In a large mixing bowl, stir together cornmeal, flour, sugar, baking soda, baking powder, buttermilk, salt, chiles, corn, eggs, and ¼ cup of olive oil. Only stir until everything is barely but evenly combined (no flour streaks). Some lumps are OK.

Add 1 tablespoon of olive oil to the skillet and use a paper towel to coat the bottom and sides. Pour the batter into the skillet and top with shredded cheese. Bake in the oven for 45–50 minutes or until the cheese on top begins to brown. Remove from oven and allow to cool.

Serve wedges at room temperature directly from the skillet. I like mine with hot sauce.

BUTTERMILK CORNBREAD

TOTAL TIME: 30 minutes

EQUIPMENT: 10-inch skillet

SERVES: 4 as a side dish

INGREDIENTS:

3 strips bacon

1 cup yellow cornmeal

1 cup all-purpose flour

⅓ cup sugar

½ tsp baking soda

1½ tsp baking powder

1½ tsp salt

1 cup buttermilk

¼ cup extra virgin olive oil

2 eggs, beaten

The first time I had cornbread was in a diner in New Jersey with my uncle. Seems out of place, no? I was about four, so most things were new to me. The guy behind the counter cut a large cornbread muffin in half, toasted it, drizzled it with melted butter, and gave it to me. I smiled. I had no clue that I was about to consume the deep South. Turns out, it was good.

—Howie

Preheat the oven to 375°F. Place the bacon into the skillet and heat over medium heat. Cook the bacon to desired level of crispiness and remove from the skillet. Eat the bacon. Keep the bacon fat in the skillet over a low heat.

While the bacon is frying, in a large mixing bowl, whisk together cornmeal, flour, sugar, baking soda, baking powder, and salt. In another mixing bowl, whisk together buttermilk, olive oil, and eggs. Stir the wet ingredients into the dry ingredients. Only stir until everything is barely combined (no flour streaks). Some lumps are OK.

Raise the skillet to medium heat. Pour batter into the skillet and fry until the very edges begin to appear brown, about 2–3 minutes. Transfer the skillet to the oven. Bake for 25–30 minutes, or until a toothpick pierced into the center of the cornbread comes out dry. Let the cornbread rest for 10 minutes.

Cut into wedges and serve from the skillet.

ROASTED POLENTA

TOTAL TIME: 1 hour

EQUIPMENT: 10-inch skillet

SERVES: 6

INGREDIENTS:

1 cup polenta or coarse cornmeal

3 cups water, hot from the tap

¾ cup whole milk, warmed

½ tsp salt

¼ tsp black pepper

¼ cup Parmesan cheese, grated or shredded

2 Tbsp butter

> Imagine fresh cornbread slathered with butter. Now imagine it slathered with butter and stuffed with cheese. Now imagine it slathered with butter, stuffed with cheese, and melting in your mouth with the silky texture of rice pudding. Actually, there's no need to imagine. Just make this polenta.
>
> —Greg

Preheat the oven to 350°F. Add water, milk, salt, and pepper into unheated skillet. Slowly pour polenta into skillet, using a whisk to mix the polenta into the water and prevent lumps.

Once the polenta is mixed into the liquid, roast, uncovered, for 50 minutes. Remove from oven and stir the polenta with a fork. Return to the oven for another 10 minutes.

Remove from oven. Stir butter and cheese into polenta until fully melted and incorporated. Sprinkle with additional grated Parmesan cheese and serve immediately. If you're feeling crazy, top it with Sunday Gravy from page 137!

CREAMY CHEWY MAC AND CHEESE

TOTAL TIME: 1 hour

EQUIPMENT: 10-inch skillet

SERVES: 6–8

INGREDIENTS:

1 lb dry macaroni or small shells

3 quarts water

3 Tbsp plus 1½ tsp salt

3 cups sharp cheddar cheese, shredded

2 eggs

¾ cup heavy cream

1 cup milk

1 cup sour cream

½ tsp ground black pepper

½ tsp garlic powder

½ tsp onion powder

½ tsp chipotle powder (optional)

1 Tbsp, plus 1 tsp extra virgin olive oil

⅓ cup breadcrumbs

> My kids love mac and cheese. They adore it. That Day-Glo orange, boxed icon comes in popular cartoon character shapes, making it an even bigger weeknight treat! That said, this homespun recipe is a different character altogether, is never confused with the supermarket version, and makes my kids smile without being a cartoon.
>
> —Howie

Preheat the oven to 375°F. In a large pot, bring water to a rolling boil over high heat. Add pasta and 3 tablespoons of the salt. Cook for 10 minutes, stirring occasionally to ensure the pasta does not stick to the pot. Drain the pasta in a colander, and rinse with cold water to stop it from cooking further. Be sure the pasta is drained completely. In a large mixing bowl, mix together 2 cups of the shredded cheese, eggs, cream, milk, sour cream, the remaining 2 teaspoons of salt, and the spices. Add in the drained pasta and mix throughout.

Coat the bottom of the skillet with a very thin layer of olive oil. Pour the pasta mixture into the skillet, mix the remaining cup of cheese with breadcrumbs. Top the casserole with the breadcrumb/cheese mixture and drizzle with olive oil. Place the skillet into the oven and bake for 40–45 minutes. The cheese on top should be bubbly and starting to brown. If the cheese doesn't brown slightly, you can turn on the broiler for one minute.

Try to include some of the chewy top with each spooned serving.

BUTTER BEANS "GIGANTES"

TOTAL TIME: 3 hours

EQUIPMENT: 12-inch skillet, with lid

SERVES: 6

INGREDIENTS:

2 15-oz cans butter beans (or large lima beans), rinsed

4 Tbsp extra virgin olive oil

1 onion, minced

4 cloves garlic, minced

1 carrot, minced

2 stalks celery, minced

2 large tomatoes, chopped

2 Tbsp tomato paste

2 Tbsp red wine vinegar

¼ cup chopped parsley

½ tsp red chile flakes

½ tsp salt

Preheat the oven to 350°F. Add 3 tablespoons of oil to skillet over medium heat. When the oil begins to shimmer, add onion and sauté for 3–4 minutes until the onion starts to brown around the edges. Add the garlic, carrot, and celery, continuing to sauté for another 5–6 minutes.

Add tomatoes, tomato paste, red wine vinegar, parsley, chile flakes, and salt. Stir to combine, cover with a lid, and place in oven for 20 minutes.

Uncover the skillet and add the beans. Replace the lid and place in the oven for 30 minutes.

Remove the lid and turn the oven up to 425°F. Cook for an additional 10–15 minutes, until the top begins to dry out.

Drizzle the top with the remaining 1 tablespoon of olive oil and serve.

WHITE BEAN STEW

TOTAL TIME: 40 minutes

EQUIPMENT: 12-inch skillet, with lid

SERVES: 6

INGREDIENTS:

¼ cup plus 2 Tbsp extra virgin olive oil

1 small onion, diced

2 garlic cloves, minced

1 15-oz can of tomatoes, crushed

2½ cups vegetable broth

2 15-oz cans cannellini or white navy beans, rinsed and drained

2 sprigs rosemary

½ tsp salt

¼ tsp ground black pepper

2 big handfuls baby arugula

> My wife and I spent a brisk and beautiful February vacation in the heart of Tuscany. We drove around the countryside, stopped off at some vineyards, and bought a case of freshly pressed olive oil. When I want to remember this trip, I could take a look at the photos, or reminisce with my lovely wife over a bottle of Barolo. But why bother with all of that, when this amazing dish says it all? Alright, maybe do all three!
>
> —Howie

Heat the skillet over medium heat. Add the olive oil and when it begins to shimmer, add onion to the skillet and sauté. When the onions start to turn translucent, after 6–8 minutes, add the garlic and continue to sauté for an additional minute. Slowly pour in the tomatoes and broth. Bring the mixture to a boil and lower the heat to low.

Stir in the beans, rosemary sprigs, salt, and pepper and simmer for 30 minutes. Remove the skillet from the heat, remove the rosemary sprigs, and stir the arugula into the stew until it wilts completely. Serve hot with No-Knead Crusty Italian Bread from page 208.

FRENCH ONION SOUP FOR TWO

TOTAL TIME: 1 hour, 40 minutes

EQUIPMENT: 8-inch skillet

SERVES: 2

INGREDIENTS:

2 Tbsp butter

2 Tbsp extra virgin olive oil

2 large white, yellow, or red onions, cut into ⅛-inch strips across the grain

2 tsp all-purpose flour

¼ cup dry red wine

2 cups beef stock or broth

2 Tbsp soy sauce

3 sprigs thyme

½ tsp salt

¼ tsp ground black pepper

7 ½-inch baguette slices,

5 oz Gruyere cheese, shredded

> My parents love French onion soup, and as much as I love them, whenever they had it at home, I ran the other way. I like onions, don't get me wrong, but that's it? It's an onion soup? A bowl full of onion? So, along came that day in culinary school when we were to learn how to make French onion soup. I wasn't looking forward to it. At all. Perhaps it was the pressure to please, maybe it was a search for childhood redemption, or was it a little of both? Well, I made the perfect French onion soup. Here it is.
>
> —Howie

Heat the skillet over medium heat. Add butter and 1 tablespoon of olive oil to the skillet and allow the butter to melt. Add the onion strips to the skillet, making sure they separate from each other. Sauté the onions until they begin to soften, about 5–7 minutes

Lower the heat to low and continue to sauté the onions for 45 minutes, stirring occasionally. You're looking for the onions to become very soft and turn light brown in color.

Preheat the oven to 400°F.

Sprinkle flour on top of the onions and mix them around to distribute the flour. Pour in the wine, stock, or broth, soy sauce, thyme sprigs, salt and pepper. Turn the heat to low and simmer, uncovered, for 25 minutes. Remove the skillet from the heat.

Drizzle the baguette slices with 1 tablespoon olive oil and toast them in the oven for 7–9 minutes, or until golden brown. Remove the toasted bread, turn your oven to broil and set a rack 6 inches from the broiler.

Place a layer of the toasted baguette slices on the surface of the soup and top with a generous layer of the shredded cheese. Place the skillet under the broiler until the cheese is melted and golden brown. Remove the skillet from the broiler and serve immediately.

TWICE-COOKED FIDEO

TOTAL TIME: 30 minutes

EQUIPMENT: 12-inch skillet, with lid

SERVES: 6–8

INGREDIENTS:

2 Tbsp extra virgin olive oil

1 12-oz package of coil fideo

2 cloves garlic, minced

2 cups water, divided

3 Tbsp tomato paste

1½ tsp salt

The Greek side of my family is loud, loving, chaotic, and a bit crazy. Memories of family reunions in the park include old men drinking bathtub ouzo out of thimbles, the kids running wild, and that spread on the picnic table. There were heaps of Spanikopita and Dolmades, baklava that hurt your teeth just from smelling it, but—most importantly—the Fideo. I think that I ate myself sick every time.

—Greg

Preheat the oven to 350°F. Add 2 teaspoons of the oil to the skillet over medium heat.

When the oil begins to shimmer, add half of the coiled fideo to your cast-iron skillet. Let the coils fry until parts become lightly brown, about 2–3 min. Flip the coils and brown the other side. Keep an eye on the noodles that break off from the coils, as they will brown more quickly.

Remove broken noodle fragments and coils from the skillet. Add 2 teaspoons of fresh oil, and repeat for the second half of the bag. Remove the second batch of fried noodles. Into the empty skillet, add another 1 teaspoon of olive oil and all the garlic. Cook until fragrant, about 30 seconds. Add 1½ cups water, tomato paste, and salt, and bring to a simmer, stirring to break up the tomato paste.

When the sauce is smooth, add all the fried noodles back into the skillet. Cover the skillet and place in the oven for 15 minutes.

Remove skillet from oven. Over medium heat, add ½ cup water and 1 teaspoon of olive oil. Gently stir the noodles to break up the last of the coils. Cook for 5 minutes, stirring occasionally until the water is gone from the pan, and the noodles are evenly moist.

Serve hot.

PORKY WHITE BREAD "STUFFING"

TOTAL TIME: 1 hour, 20 minutes

EQUIPMENT: 12-inch skillet

SERVES: 8–10

INGREDIENTS:

1½-lb loaf crusty bread, cut
    into 1-inch cubes

4 Tbsp extra virgin olive oil

1 Tbsp butter

1 large onion, diced

3 stalks celery, diced

2 tsp salt

½ tsp ground black pepper

½ tsp garlic powder

½ tsp chile powder

1 Tbsp sage, chopped

1 4-oz can of roasted green chiles

2 Tbsp parsley, roughly chopped

¼ lb ham, diced

1 lb smoked Andouille sausage (about 4 links), diced

1 large egg

4 cups chicken, turkey, or ham stock, cooled

½ cup milk

> Years ago, when I started to host Thanksgiving dinner, my anxiety was focused on the "stuffing." (I use quotes because it's not actually stuffed into a bird!) I grew up on the boxed stove-top version, which I adored in all of its faux glory! Can I somehow be loyal to the memory of this holiday staple and yet firmly plant my own flag? Dear reader, I present my case below.
>
> —Howie

Preheat the oven to broil with one rack 6 inches under the broiler and another rack in the center. Place bread cubes on a sheet pan in a single layer and drizzle with 2 tablespoons of olive oil. Broil the bread cubes for 5–6 minutes. You're looking for something close to morning toast. Remove the toasted bread and reset the oven to 375°F.

In the skillet, melt butter with the remaining olive oil. Over medium heat, sauté onion, celery, 1 teaspoon of salt, and the remaining seasonings until the onion is translucent, about 6–8 minutes. Transfer the contents to a large mixing bowl. To this bowl, mix in the chiles, parsley, ham, Andouille, and toast cubes. Pour this mixture into the skillet and make sure it is evenly distributed across the surface.

In the same mixing bowl, whisk the eggs, stock, milk, and the remaining 1 teaspoon of salt. Slowly pour the liquid evenly over the mixture in the skillet, being sure that some of the liquid reaches most, if not all, of the bread. Use the back of a wooden spoon or spatula to compress the whole mixture to ensure that the liquid is evenly distributed.

Move the skillet to the center rack of the oven. Bake for 50–60 minutes, until the top is beginning to brown and get crusty. Allow the "stuffing" to rest for 10–15 minutes before serving. Or, allow to cool completely and reheat for ten minutes at 350°F.

NO-PORKY CORNBREAD "STUFFING"

TOTAL TIME: overnight, plus 1 hour, 20 minutes

EQUIPMENT: 10-inch skillet

SERVES: 8–10

Sometimes there's room at the table for a no-porky version of things. Not often, but it happens. I kid. I love this cornbread "stuffing" in all of its mushrooms' umami glory. Hailing from the Southern US, one may expect a cornbread "stuffing" to reflect much of the same flavor elements as the porky version above, but here, we take more of a New England approach, if only to try and forget about the lack of pig. Again, I kid. Do this, now.

—Howie

INGREDIENTS:

1 loaf Buttermilk Cornbread, from page 189 (without bacon for truly vegetarian)

4 Crispy, Flaky Biscuits, from page 29

2 Tbsp butter

2 Tbsp extra virgin olive oil

14 oz cremini, white button, or shiitake mushrooms, stemmed and thinly sliced

3 ribs celery, diced

1 green bell pepper, diced

2 tsp salt

1 tsp ground black pepper

½ tsp onion powder

½ tsp garlic powder

2 tsp dried or fresh thyme leaves

5 scallions, thinly sliced

2 Tbsp parsley, roughly chopped

2 large eggs

3 cups vegetable or mushroom stock, cooled

Leave the cornbread and biscuits on the counter, uncovered, overnight to dry out. Preheat the oven to 350°F.

In the skillet, melt butter over medium heat and sauté mushrooms until they give off their water and start to brown, about 10 minutes. Transfer the mushrooms to a large mixing bowl. To the skillet, add 1 tablespoon of the oil, celery, bell pepper, salt, and seasonings except for scallions and parsley. Continue to sauté until the celery is almost translucent, about 6–8 minutes. Transfer the skillet contents to the mixing bowl and allow to cool for a few minutes.

To this bowl, mix in the scallions and parsley, then roughly crumble cornbread and biscuits on top. In a separate bowl, whisk together eggs and stock. Pour the stock mixture into the bread mixture. Stir to combine until the liquid is fully absorbed.

Drizzle olive oil into the skillet and spread across the surfaces with a paper towel or pastry brush. Pour the mixture into the skillet, gently pressing to ensure everything fits in one solid layer. Place the skillet onto the center rack of the oven and bake for 50–60 minutes until the top is slightly browned and crusty. Allow the "stuffing" to rest for 10–15 minutes before serving. Or, allow to cool completely and reheat for ten minutes at 350°F.

BUBBE'S TRANSYLVANIAN LATKES

TOTAL TIME: 2 hours

EQUIPMENT: 12-inch skillet

SERVES: 8–10

INGREDIENTS:

5 lb russet or Yukon Gold
   potatoes

6 eggs, beaten

1 medium onion

vegetable oil for frying

1 Tbsp salt

¼ tsp white pepper

> If you've ever been to a Chanukah party, you've probably been given a greasy, heavy hash brown that was only salvaged by drowning it in a pool of sour cream and applesauce. Oy, what a travesty! Along with volumes of dirty jokes, my Transylvanian great-grandmother passed down the recipe for this light, amazingly tasty latke. Often compared to donut holes or beignets, they are a lot of work, but worth every scraped knuckle.
>
> —Greg

Fill a small bowl halfway with water. Grate the potatoes into the water, using the "grater" side of your box grater (this is the side with the outward protruding holes with spiky edges on all sides). When your bowl fills, empty the potatoes and water into a large pot or bowl. Refill your grating bowl with fresh water, and continue until all potatoes are grated.

Scoop the grated potatoes into a thin-meshed sieve and run under water for 20–30 seconds until the water runs through clear. This removes much of the potato starch and leads to a fluffier latke. Dump the rinsed potatoes into a bowl or pot, again covering with water.

Grated, rinsed potatoes can sit under water for up to 6 hours. Beginning with the next step, you need to move quickly.

Using a grater or food processor, grate the onion into a bowl, reserving all the onion and liquid. Using a fine-meshed sieve, remove the potatoes from the water and press them with your hand to remove most of the water. Place dried potatoes into a bowl. Add onion, eggs, salt, and pepper and stir well.

Pour enough oil in the skillet to about 1 inch in depth. Heat the oil to 360°F over medium heat. If you do not have a thermometer, one handy trick is to use a wooden chopstick, like the kind you get with Chinese take out. As the oil heats, touch the tip of the chopstick to the bottom of the skillet at an angle. Once you see bubbles forming around the entirety of the submerged chopstick, the oil is ready.

Scoop out some of the potato/egg mixture and lightly press to remove some, but not all, the moisture. Use a large spoon to form some of this mixture into a football shape, and place in the hot oil.

Latkes will float in the oil. Turn when the submerged half becomes golden brown. Remove when entire latke is golden brown, about 8–10 minutes total.

Serve traditionally with sour cream and applesauce, though cranberry sauce is a personal favorite accompaniment.

NO-KNEAD CRUSTY ITALIAN BREAD

TOTAL TIME: 3 hours, 35 minutes

EQUIPMENT: 8-inch skillet

SERVES: 6–8

INGREDIENTS:

¾ Tbsp rapid rise yeast or
   1 Tbsp active dry yeast

3 cups all-purpose or bread
   flour

2 tsp salt

1 tsp sugar

1 cup water, warm from the
   tap

3 Tbsp extra virgin olive oil

Cooking spray

When I was in culinary school, I decided that becoming a chef was not in the cards. With two small kids, the hours would have been my demise. However, all was not lost. The lessons on bread changed my life. It takes mere moments to put together dough, and then, no effort to produce something you would have otherwise spent 10 times more cash on. Need I say more? Bake bread. This one is a gem.

—Howie

Note about yeast: If you're using active dry yeast, bloom the yeast in the cup of water for 5 minutes before adding to the dry ingredients.

Note about flour: If you use bread flour, the inside of the bread will have a chewier consistency.

In the bowl of a stand mixer, whisk together the rapid rise yeast (if using), flour, salt, and sugar. With the dough hook attached, on the slowest speed, mix in the water and 2 tablespoons of the olive oil. When the flour is fully incorporated into a dough, increase the speed by one.

When the dough begins to come away from the sides of the bowl, stop the mixer, remove the dough hook, and cover the bowl with plastic wrap and allow to ferment on the counter for 2 hours. The dough will become bubbly and much larger in size.

Drizzle the remaining 1 tablespoon of olive oil in the skillet and coat the bottom and insides using a paper towel. Pour the dough into the skillet and allow it to settle to the edges by gently shaking the pan. Spray cooking spray across the top of the dough and cover with plastic wrap. Set aside for an hour, or until the dough doubles in size. After about 45 minutes, preheat the oven to 425°F.

Remove the plastic wrap from the dough and transfer the skillet to the oven. Bake for 35 minutes. Remove the skillet from the oven and transfer the bread from the skillet to a wire rack on the counter. Allow the bread to rest for an hour before cutting.

Serve with whatever you would imagine bread to be served with! Eat it by itself! It's delicious!

HAPPY ENDINGS

GRANDMA'S SWEET KUGEL

TOTAL TIME: 1 hour, 10 minutes

EQUIPMENT: 10-inch skillet

SERVES: 4–6

INGREDIENTS:

12 oz wide egg noodles

4 tsp butter or vegetable shortening

3 large eggs, beaten

¾ cup crushed pineapple, drained

¾ cup raisins

8 maraschino cherries, roughly chopped

½ cup sugar

4 tsp cinnamon

Featuring canned pineapple and maraschino cherries, this recipe screams 1950s American cuisine. Probably because that's exactly what it is. But don't be put off—it's as delicious now as it was when my Grandma first threw it together.

—Greg

Cook the egg noodles in salted water according to the package directions. Drain and rinse the noodles with cold water to stop them from cooking further. Store them in a large mixing bowl.

Preheat the oven to 350°F. In a small bowl, stir together eggs, pineapple, raisins, cherries, sugar, and cinnamon. Pour the egg mixture over the noodles and stir to combine and distribute raisins and cherries evenly.

Place the butter or vegetable shortening in the skillet over medium heat for 1–2 minutes, until melted and shimmering. Adjust heat to medium-low and pour the noodle mixture into the skillet. Using a spatula, push down on the noodles to get rid of any gaps and to spread evenly.

Cook on stovetop for 5 minutes, then move to the heated oven. Kugel should bake, uncovered, for 15 minutes. Finally, turn the oven to broil and brown the top of the kugel for about 2 minutes.

Allow the kugel to cool for 30–45 minutes. Unmold it from pan by placing a large plate over the top of the skillet and turning the skillet upside down. Serve slightly warm or at room temperature.

ONE BIG COOKIE

TOTAL TIME: 35 minutes

EQUIPMENT: 10-inch skillet

SERVES: 4–6 (or 8–10, if you're feeling generous)

This recipe allows you to make 4 dinner plate-sized cookies.

INGREDIENTS:

1 cup old fashioned oats

1¼ cups all-purpose flour

1 tsp baking soda

1 tsp salt

1 cup (2 sticks) butter

¾ cup sugar

¾ cup light brown sugar

2 tsp vanilla extract

2 large eggs

2 cups chocolate chips, milk, semi-sweet, or dark

Technically, this recipe will make 4 dinner plate-sized cookies. But, you'll likely not need that many in one sitting. You may want that many, but since you're going to want to recreate the magic within the next day, you should save half of the dough in the fridge. Or, make them all and turn a good night into a great one.

—Howie

Preheat oven to 375°F. Grind old-fashioned oats in a food processor until they are very finely ground, as close to regular flour as possible.

In a mixing bowl, whisk together flours, baking soda, and salt. Cream butter and sugars together in a stand mixer or with an electric hand mixer until creamy. Add eggs and vanilla on low speed and mix until well blended. Add half of dry ingredients until just incorporated. Add remaining dry ingredients and mix until well blended. Stir in chocolate chips.

Split the dough into four even portions, rolling it into balls. Take three of the balls, cover them in plastic wrap, and store in the refrigerator for later batches. Each ball will make one big cookie.

Line the bottom of the skillet with parchment paper. Place one of the balls of cookie dough into the prepared skillet. Spread dough out with clean fingers until it is ¾-inch to 1-inch thick, keeping a circular shape as much as possible.

Bake for 9–15 minutes. Watch the cookie closely after 9 minutes to ensure the center cooks but the edges do not burn. Allow cookie to cool for 10 minutes before gently removing from the skillet. Let the cookie fully cool on a cooling rack before handling further.

Line the skillet with new parchment paper and repeat with the remaining dough.

APPLE CRISP

TOTAL TIME: 1 hour

EQUIPMENT: 10-inch skillet

SERVES: 8-10

INGREDIENTS:

Crisp Topping:

¾ cup all-purpose flour

½ tsp cinnamon

⅓ cup sugar

⅓ cup brown sugar

¾ cup butter, cold, cut into ½-inch cubes

¾ cup rolled oats

Apple Mixture:

3 Tbsp sugar

½ tsp cinnamon

7-8 apples (Braeburn, Jonagold, Pippin, Granny Smith, etc.), peeled, cored, cut into bite sized pieces

Do you know the difference between a crisp and a crumble? Well, do you? To be honest, I didn't either, until we started to write this recipe. Oats. Crisps have oats. So, it's a breakfast food. Right?
—Howie

Preheat oven to 375°F. Prepare the skillet by thoroughly buttering the bottom and sides.

Add flour, cinnamon, sugar, and brown sugar to the bowl of a food processor and pulse 5-6 times. Add half of the butter and pulse 5-6 times to combine. Use a fork to ensure that the ingredients are evenly distributed. Add the remaining butter and pulse 5-6 times. Pour contents into a large bowl. Add oats and mix with clean hands until topping resembles coarse crumbs. Place topping mixture in refrigerator until the base of the crisp is ready.

Combine sugar and cinnamon in a small bowl. Layer apples and cinnamon sugar mixture in the skillet.

Remove topping from refrigerator. Mix again gently with your hands. Distribute the topping on the apple mixture evenly. Bake 30-45 minutes until topping is golden brown and apples are tender. Serve warm with ice cream.

ALMOND-CRUSTED APPLE PIE

TOTAL TIME: 90 minutes

EQUIPMENT: 10- to 12-inch skillet

SERVES: 8–10

INGREDIENTS:

Crust:

1½ cups almond flour

1 Tbsp arrowroot powder

½ tsp table salt

1 Tbsp canola or vegetable oil

2 Tbsp honey

1 egg white

Filling:

½ cup apple juice

¼ cup honey

1 lemon, juiced

1 Tbsp arrowroot powder

1½ tsp cinnamon

2 Tbsp canola or vegetable oil

7–8 apples (Braeburn, Jonagold, Pippin, Granny Smith, etc.), peeled, cored, cut into bite-sized pieces

To make the crust, combine all ingredients except for the egg white in a food processor. Using the metal blade, pulse until you see clumps of moistened dough forming, about ten 1-second pulses. Remove dough to a bowl and form into a single ball. Wrap ball in plastic wrap and place in freezer for 30 minutes, until firm.

To prepare the filling, in a small mixing bowl combine apple juice, honey, lemon juice, arrowroot powder, and cinnamon. Whisk to mix evenly.

Heat oven to 500°F.

Place skillet over medium-high heat and add oil. When the oil begins to shimmer, add apples. Sauté apples for 5 minutes, turning them occasionally to brown all sides. Remove from heat and pour apple juice mixture into the skillet, stirring to coat all apple slices.

To assemble the pie, dust two 16-inch pieces of parchment paper with almond flour. Place chilled dough in the center of one piece, covering the dough with the second piece. Roll the dough into a 12-inch-diameter disk, keeping your rolling pin on top of the parchment paper. (The dough will be too sticky to come into direct contact with your rolling pin.) Peel off the top piece of parchment paper. Gently fold the dough over the apple-filled skillet dough-side down, paper-side up. Peel off the second piece of parchment paper.

Brush egg white over the top of the dough. Place skillet in oven for 6–8 minutes, until slightly browned. Turn off the oven, but leave the skillet in there for another 10–15 minutes, until golden brown. Remove from oven and allow to rest for at least 15 minutes.

Served immediately or at room temperature with whipped cream or vanilla ice cream.

WE HAVE TO MAKE THIS CHOCOLATE POUND CAKE

TOTAL TIME: 1½ hours

EQUIPMENT: 8-inch skillet

SERVES: 6–8

It's your duty. You must. Your friends will love you even more than they do right now. You'll be smarter, faster, and more capable of anything you wish to do. After making this cake, you will be superior in every way. Also, you will be full. Pound cakes are heavy.

—Howie

INGREDIENTS:

½ cup (1 stick) unsalted butter

1 cup sugar

1½ cups flour

½ tsp salt

¼ tsp baking soda

4 oz chocolate chips (semisweet, milk chocolate, or dark)

1 tsp vanilla extract

2 large eggs

1 cup buttermilk

Preheat oven to 325°F. Coat the inside of the skillet with cooking spray or butter.

Using a stand mixer with the paddle attachment, mix butter and sugar on medium speed until very light in color, about 4–5 minutes. In a small bowl, whisk together flour, salt, and baking soda. Set aside.

Place chocolate chips in a microwave safe bowl. Melt on low power (20%) in 1 minute increments, stirring after each minute, until melted. Add vanilla and melted chocolate to the creamed butter. Beat until well mixed using a rubber spatula to push the mixture down the sides of the bowl, as needed.

Add eggs, one at a time. Beat well after adding each egg.

Add one-third of the flour mixture and mix on low until just incorporated. Add half of the buttermilk and mix until smooth. Add one-third of flour mixture and remaining buttermilk and mix until just incorporated. Add remaining flour mixture and mix until smooth. Continue to use a rubber spatula to push the mixture down the sides of the bowl, as needed, to ensure batter is smooth.

Pour batter into skillet until two-thirds full and level the top with the rubber spatula.

Bake 30–45 minutes. A cake tester or toothpick pierced into the center should come out clean. Allow the cake to cool for 30 minutes. Serve directly from the skillet, and top with powdered sugar, ice cream, or whipped cream.

CHOCOLATE CHIP BREAD PUDDING

TOTAL TIME: 1 hour

EQUIPMENT: 10-inch skillet

SERVES: 8–10

INGREDIENTS:

3 large eggs

1½ cups heavy cream

½ cup granulated sugar

2 Tbsp vanilla extract

1 tsp cinnamon

1-lb loaf crusty bread, 1-inch slices

Butter for buttering bread

¾ cup milk chocolate chips

> When you think of bread pudding, the words "soggy" and "heavy" often come to mind. This bread pudding is different. It's light, airy, coco-licious, and it'll knock your socks off. It's from the mind of my lovely wife, Jessica. So, please tell her I said so. It's become hard to wear socks around the house without raising suspicions.
>
> —Howie

Preheat the oven to broil with one rack 6 inches below the broiler, and another rack in the center of the oven.

In a medium bowl, whisk together the eggs, heavy cream, sugar, vanilla, and cinnamon. Butter each slice of bread on one side, generously. Broil the slices for 3–5 minutes to dry out the bread. Golden brown is OK, but don't allow the bread to get to dark brown. Remove bread from the oven and let the toast slices cool for 2–3 minutes. Cut the bread into 1-inch cubes (or you can tear it with your hands). Preheat the oven to 350°F.

Add half of the bread cubes to the bottom of the skillet. Sprinkle ¼ cup of the chocolate chips over the first layer. Layer in the second half of the bread cubes. Sprinkle ¼ cup of chocolate chips over the second layer. Slowly pour the egg custard evenly over the bread cubes and chocolate, being sure that some of the custard reaches most (if not all) of the bread. Sprinkle the final ¼ cup of chocolate chips over the top of the bread pudding. Use the back of a wooden spoon to compress the bread pudding mixture, to ensure that the custard is evenly distributed.

Place the skillet on the center rack of the oven and bake for 30 minutes. Let the bread pudding cool for 10 minutes. Serve with ice cream or whipped cream to taste.

WORKOUT TO EARN THIS BROWNIE

TOTAL TIME: 1 hour

EQUIPMENT: 8-inch skillet

SERVES: 8–10

INGREDIENTS:

9 Tbsp butter

¾ cup cocoa

1 cup sugar

¼ tsp salt

¾ tsp vanilla

2 eggs

¼ cup all-purpose flour

No, I'm not giving you a directive, trying to suggest something rude, or even mandating exercise before you get to have a sweet treat! This brownie truly does require a workout. The whipping. Oh, the whipping! The results are amazing, however, and the hard work pays off in the end. Best. Brownie. Ever. Then, nap.

—Howie

Preheat oven to 375°F. Line the inside of the skillet with a layer of aluminum foil, covering the bottom and all sides.

Melt butter in the microwave for 60–90 seconds. Combine cocoa, sugar, and salt in a large bowl. Add melted butter to cocoa mixture and stir well so the butter cools. Add vanilla, then the eggs, incorporating one at a time.

Workout part 1: Mix well with a wooden spoon until batter is very smooth and glossy, about one minute. Taking your time to get the batter very smooth is critical.

Workout part 2: Add flour and mix until incorporated. Mix batter very well with swift, fast strokes, counting to 75 slowly.

Pour batter into prepared skillet. Use your wooden spoon to spread batter evenly in the skillet.

Transfer the skillet to the oven and bake for 20 minutes. Let the brownies cool at least 30 minutes before removing from the pan to serve with ice cream or on their own.

MIXED BERRY COBBLER

TOTAL TIME: 40 minutes

EQUIPMENT: 8-inch skillet

SERVES: 6–8

> Growing up, I wasn't a fan of fruit-based desserts. But, if you had told me that I could involve biscuits, I would've sung a different tune! Biscuits make everything better.
> —Howie

INGREDIENTS:

- 1 16-oz bag of frozen mixed berries
- ½ cup light brown sugar
- 1 Tbsp cornstarch
- 1 cup all-purpose flour
- 1 tsp baking powder
- ¼ tsp salt
- 6 Tbsp unsalted butter, cold, cut into ½ inch cubes
- ⅜ cup buttermilk
- 1 Tbsp sugar

Preheat the oven to 425°F.

Mix berries, brown sugar, and cornstarch in a mixing bowl. Pour berry mixture into skillet and roast in the oven for 15 minutes. Stir halfway through to ensure berries are evenly warmed.

To prepare the dough, in a large mixing bowl, mix flour, baking powder, and salt. Add the butter cubes and incorporate into the flour mixture with a pastry cutter or squeeze with your fingertips until the pieces of butter are consistently smaller than peas. Add buttermilk and mix well with your fingers until dough forms.

Remove warm berry mixture from the oven. Gently place dollops of dough around the surface of the berry mixture. Use a spoon to sprinkle sugar on top of cobbler topping.

Bake cobbler in the oven 20–25 minutes until the topping is golden brown. Serve warm with ice cream or whipped cream.

BANANAS FAUX-STER

TOTAL TIME: 5 minutes

EQUIPMENT: 8- to 10-inch skillet

SERVES: 2–4

INGREDIENTS:

¼ cup butter

½ cup dark brown sugar, packed

¼ cup heavy cream

1 banana, very yellow, peeled and cut in half widthwise and then each half lengthwise

¼ cup bourbon, 101 proof

⅛ tsp ground cinnamon

> Traditionally, bananas foster is a made with rum. Ahoy, matey! If one wants a real fireworks show, one uses a high-proof rum, something in the neighborhood of 150 proof! But, what if you don't have rum? Well, I had a dream in which I combined my love of bourbon and my desire for this delectable dessert. When I awoke, I made it.
> —Howie

Heat the skillet over medium heat. Melt the butter and sugar together. When the sugar is dissolved in the butter, after about 2 minutes, add the cream and stir it through.

Place the four banana segments in the caramel sauce in the skillet. Spoon some of the caramel on top of each banana segment. Raise the heat to medium-high and allow the caramel to bubble rapidly. Move the skillet off of the heat, drizzle the bourbon around the pan, then move the skillet back on the heat.

Using a stick lighter or a long match, light the skillet on fire. Technically, you're setting the bourbon fumes aflame. This beautiful fire will go out once the alcohol has burned off. When that occurs, sprinkle cinnamon atop the bananas. The sauce will tighten quickly as it cools.

Serve the bananas topped with caramel sauce and a scoop of ice cream.

PINEAPPLE UPSIDE-DOWN CAKE

TOTAL TIME: 1 hour, 30 minutes

EQUIPMENT: 8- to 10-inch skillet

SERVES: 8–10

INGREDIENTS:

Topping:

1 20-oz can pineapple rings, drained and sliced into quarters.

6 Tbsp unsalted butter

¾ cup light brown sugar

Cake:

1½ cups all-purpose flour

2 tsp baking powder

½ tsp cinnamon

½ tsp salt

6 Tbsp unsalted butter

1 cup sugar

2 large eggs

½ tsp vanilla

¼ tsp almond extract

½ cup milk

When I was a young Boy Scout, there was an older man—let's call him Mr. Baldy because I think that may have been his actual name—who sometimes joined us. On several camping trips, he would arrive with a ready pineapple upside-down cake, cooked under his Chevrolet's hood by the heat of his exhaust manifold. Here's an approximation of that surprisingly moist and delicious cake, minus the airborne carcinogens.

—Greg

Preheat oven to 350°F. Heat the skillet over medium-low heat. Melt the butter, then add light brown sugar and cook until the sugar dissolves, about 3–5 minutes. Remove pan from heat. Lay pineapple slices gently on the butter/sugar mixture in a circular pattern. Start with the outside circle first and work your way in. Set skillet aside while you make the cake batter.

Mix dry ingredients in a medium bowl and set aside. Beat butter and sugar with an electric mixer until light and creamy (approximately 5 minutes). Add eggs one at a time, mixing gently. Add extracts and beat until eggs and extracts are well incorporated. Add half of the dry mixture and half of the milk and beat slowly until just incorporated. Add remaining dry mixture and milk. Mix until well incorporated.

With a rubber spatula or large spoon, gently spoon batter evenly over the topping. It is important not to "break" through to the topping mixture, so work slowly and carefully. Spread batter evenly with a rubber spatula.

Bake for 45 minutes or until cake is golden brown and a tester comes out clean. Let cake cool in skillet for 30 minutes. To remove cake from pan, run a knife along the edge of the skillet and then flip the cake onto a large plate.

THE GREAT OUTDOORS

For the next seven recipes, here is a suggested model for setting up a campfire cooking environment. To accomplish what we recommend, you will need a campfire grill, unless there is a grill rack built into the fire rings at your campsite.

On the camping day, 30 minutes before dinnertime, start a small fire apart from your larger campfire, or build your main campfire larger after dinner! The goal here is to create a fire that is low enough in height to place a grill rack 5 inches above, and finally the skillet on top. Your grill rack should have its own foldout legs. Otherwise, you could place bricks or large stones on either side of the fire so that the rack sits across them, again, about 5 inches above the fire logs.

One good model is to start a fire with kindling and gradually add larger pieces of dry tree branches from the forest floor before adding just one log or two. If you successfully get the logs lit, make sure it stays lit. You may need to add a log or two as your previous logs burn to ash. The goal is to maintain blue or orange flames licking the bottom of the skillet for the duration of your cooking time. Happy camping!

—Howie

ONE PAN BREAKFAST

TOTAL TIME: 20 minutes

EQUIPMENT: 12-inch skillet

SERVES: 3–4

INGREDIENTS:

½ lb breakfast sausage links

1 Tbsp extra virgin olive oil

¼ cup water

15 cherry tomatoes

4 eggs

½ tsp salt

¼ tsp ground black pepper

You've just slept on the ground. Sure there was a suggestion of air in the camping pad, but the ground was very much present. You're creaky and sore. You unzip the tent, step outside, take a nice long stretch, and yawn. It's chilly, misty, and you smell like a campfire. Which would you rather have for breakfast, some boring trail mix or something filling and delicious to start the day off right? Yeah, that's what I thought. Enjoy!

—Howie

Place the skillet over the fire and pour in water and oil. Once the skillet begins to sputter and pop, add in the sausage. Occasionally roll the links around in the pan to brown on all sides. After 8–10 minutes, add the tomatoes to the pan. Again, roll them around the skillet occasionally for about 3 minutes, until their skin begins to blister and tear.

Move the sausage and tomatoes to one side of the skillet. Crack open each egg and carefully place the unbroken yolk and white into the skillet's open space. Sprinkle the eggs and the tomatoes with salt. The eggs will cook within 4 minutes.

Eat from the skillet. We're all friends here.

CAMPFIRE BURRITOS

TOTAL TIME: ½ hour before camping and
1½ hours during camping

EQUIPMENT: 12-inch skillet

SERVES: 6-8

INGREDIENTS:

1 30-oz can pinto beans, drained

1 9-oz can green chiles (hot or mild)

1 lb Monterey jack cheese, shredded

1 lb Chopped Pork from page 127

2 bell peppers, minced

1 large white onion, minced

1 bunch cilantro, roughly chopped

8 large flour tortillas

8 corn tortillas

½ cup extra virgin olive oil

salsa

sour cream

guacamole

The day before going camping, pack each of the first 7 ingredients in separate containers and store in the refrigerator or in a portable cooler. Remember to bring along enough spoons to serve each of the burrito components.

Place the skillet over the fire and let it get hot. Warm a tortilla on the grate over open flame or in the skillet until it's pliable, just a few seconds on each side. Fill the center of the tortilla with desired ingredients and roll burrito. It is best to tuck in both ends as you roll to ensure your filling stays inside while cooking.

Place 1 teaspoon of oil in the skillet for each burrito and let it heat up. Place the burrito(s) into the skillet, seam-side down. When the bottom is golden brown, after 3-5 minutes (depending on the heat of your fire), flip the burrito and allow the other side to brown, another 2-3 minutes.

Serve with salsa, sour cream, and guacamole.

PIZZA NACHOS

TOTAL TIME: 10 minutes

EQUIPMENT: 12-inch skillet

SERVES: 4

INGREDIENTS:

2 tsp extra virgin olive oil

10 oz tortilla chips

½ cup pepperoni, thinly sliced

12 cherry tomatoes, quartered

1 red bell pepper, thinly sliced

1 lb mozzarella cheese, shredded

3 scallions, thinly sliced

This is a real crowd pleaser for family camping trips. All the crunch of nachos, all the pepperoni of pizza, all the cheese of both. Need I say more?

Greg

Into an unheated skillet, add 2 teaspoons of oil and coat the bottom of the pan with a paper towel.

Layer half the chips on the bottom of the pan, followed by half of the toppings and cheese. Repeat to create a second layer.

Heat skillet over a low, open fire. Cook for 6–8 minutes, until the cheese is melted. While cooking, use a spatula to occasionally peek at the bottom of the nachos, making sure that the chips aren't burning.

Serve immediately.

SWEET AND SMOKY BAKED BEANS

TOTAL TIME: 40 minutes

EQUIPMENT: 8-inch skillet

SERVES: 2–3

INGREDIENTS:

2 pieces bacon, sliced into ⅛ inch strips

1 30-oz can pinto or white beans

2 Tbsp brown sugar

2 Tbsp ketchup

½ tsp mustard powder

1 Tbsp Worcestershire sauce

1–1½ cups water

There's something so iconic about sitting in front of an open fire with a pot of beans bubbling away in a cast-iron skillet. Whether served alone as a light supper, or as part of a larger barbeque, these sweet and savory beans are something I look forward to on every camping trip.

—Greg

Heat skillet over a low, open fire. When the skillet is hot, add bacon and fry until just brown and crispy, about 4–6 minutes.

Add the beans, sugar, ketchup, mustard powder, and Worcestershire sauce. Add water to cover the beans by ½ inch. Simmer for 20–30 minutes, adding water to make sure the beans do not get too dry.

Serve immediately.

FIREBALL SANDWICHES

TOTAL TIME: 10 minutes

EQUIPMENT: 12-inch skillet, with lid

SERVES: 4–6

INGREDIENTS:

1 lb ground beef

8 oz. crusty white bread, ripped into chunks

1 egg

1½ tsp salt

½ tsp ground black pepper

½ tsp cayenne, chipotle powder or red pepper flakes

1 tsp dried oregano

3 Tbsp Parmesan cheese, grated or shredded

1 Tbsp extra virgin olive oil

1 15-oz can of tomato sauce

Sandwich Rolls

> While not as traditional a camp meal as hamburgers, a meatball sandwich is actually a lot more practical. Braising the meat in sauce means that it's pretty tough to overcook—a common problem with camp hamburgers. And a meatball sandwich doesn't require you to have an ice chest full of lettuce, mayo, and other fixings. Give my spicy meatball a chance, and you'll never go back.
>
> —Greg

To make the meatball mixture, place bread chunks in a large bowl. Slowly pour water over the bread chunks until all of the bread is moistened. Using clean hands, mash the bread until it forms a paste, adding additional water if needed.

Add the beef, egg, salt, pepper, chiles, oregano, and cheese to the bowl. Using clean hands, blend until mixed evenly, though the occasional small pocket of bread will remain. Store this meatball mixture in a sealed plastic bag, inside of a chilled cooler for the trip.

To prepare at the campsite, add olive oil to cold skillet. Form meat mixture into twelve 2-inch meatballs and place them in the skillet. Cover skillet with the lid.

Heat covered skillet over a low, open fire for 10–12 minutes, until the outsides of the meatballs are fully cooked, and the bottom is slightly browned. Pour tomato sauce into the skillet, and continue to cook, uncovered, for another 20 minutes.

Serve on sandwich rolls or other bread, sprinkled with additional Parmesan cheese.

STONED CHICKEN

TOTAL TIME: 1 hour, 5 minutes

EQUIPMENT: 12-inch skillet

SERVES: 4–6

INGREDIENTS:

1 4–5 lb chicken, butterflied by
   the butcher

2 tsp salt

1 tsp ground black pepper

2 oranges, halved

Does roasting a whole chicken over a campfire seem indulgent? Yes.

—Howie

Wrap the chicken in a few layers of plastic and store it in a chilled cooler for the trip.

At the campsite, find a large stone, or two smaller ones and wrap them in aluminum foil. If you don't want to risk not finding stones, bring along two bricks from home and wrap them in the foil.

Unwrap the chicken and season both sides with salt and pepper. Add 1 tablespoon of the oil to the skillet, then place the chicken breast side down. Drizzle the remaining oil over the chicken. Place the stone(s) or bricks on top of the chicken. Heat skillet over a low, open fire for 25–30 minutes, or until the breast side skin is dark and crusty.

Remove the skillet from the fire and use sturdy tongs to carefully flip the chicken. Squeeze one whole orange's worth of juice into the skillet. Return the skillet to the fire for an additional 25 minutes. Remove the skillet from the fire and the chicken from the skillet.

Let the chicken rest, breast side up, for 10 minutes before picking the meat with a couple of forks. Serve hot with a squeeze or two of orange juice and maybe some of those Sweet and Smoky Baked Beans from page 241.

S'MORITOS

TOTAL TIME: 10 minutes

EQUIPMENT: 12-inch skillet

SERVES: 4

INGREDIENTS:

4 tsp butter

4 small wheat tortillas (often called "fajita size")

4 tsp brown sugar

1 cup mini marshmallows

2 small milk chocolate bars (1.5 oz each)

S'mores are great in theory, but in practice are frequently underwhelming. Unevenly roasted marshmallows. Cold, brittle chocolate. Enter the s'morito—a crisp tortilla shell filled with an oozing chocolate marshmallow cream.

—Greg

Heat skillet over open fire. Place about ½ teaspoon of butter in the middle of four 12-inch by 12-inch pieces of aluminum foil.

When skillet is hot, place a tortilla in the dry skillet for 20–30 seconds, until slightly brown. Flip tortilla and cook on the opposite side for 15 seconds. Tortilla should now be pliable without breaking.

Remove hot tortilla to the buttered foil. Spread ½ teaspoon of butter and 1 teaspoon of brown sugar across the middle of the tortilla. Add about 20 mini marshmallows and half of a chocolate bar.

Fold burrito tightly, making sure that both ends are tucked in. Wrap folded burrito in buttered foil. Repeat for each burrito.

Place the 4 foil packets in the skillet. Cook on one side for 2–3 minutes. Flip all the packages and cook on the other side for the same amount of time. Remove from heat, unwrap, and enjoy.

INDEX

CONVERSION CHARTS

Metric and Imperial Conversions

(These conversions are rounded for convenience)

Ingredient	Cups/Tablespoons/Teaspoons	Ounces	Grams/Milliliters
Oil	1 cup=16 tablespoons	7.5 ounces	209 grams
Cheese, shredded	1 cup	4 ounces	110 grams
Flour, all-purpose	1 cup/1 tablespoon	4.5 ounces/0.3 ounces	125 grams/8 grams
Fruit, dried	1 cup	4 ounces	120 grams
Fruits or veggies, chopped	1 cup	5 to 7 ounces	145 to 200 grams
Fruits or veggies, puréed	1 cup	8.5 ounces	245 grams
Honey or maple syrup	1 tablespoon	0.75 ounces	20 grams
Liquids: milks, water, vinegar, or juice	1 cup	8 fluid ounces	240 milliliters
Salt	1 teaspoon	0.2 ounces	6 grams
Spices: cinnamon, cloves, ginger, or nutmeg (ground)	1 teaspoon	0.2 ounces	5 milliliters

Oven Temperatures

Fahrenheit	Celcius	Gas Mark
225°	110°	¼
250°	120°	½
275°	140°	1
300°	150°	2
325°	160°	3
350°	180°	4
375°	190°	5
400°	200°	6
425°	220°	7
450°	230°	8

ABOUT THE AUTHORS

Greg Matza and Howie Southworth are the bestselling authors behind *One Pan to Rule Them All: 100 Cast-Iron Skillet Recipes for Indoors and Out*, and *Kiss My Casserole: 100 Mouthwatering Recipes Inspired By Ovens Around the World*, and *Chinese Street Food: Small Bites, Classic Recipes, and Harrowing Tales Across the Middle Kingdom.*

They first formed their creative partnership over twenty-five years ago. This dynamic duo first met during college, working at a summer camp on the University of California campus in Santa Barbara. Be jealous. They became fast friends over Sammy Davis Jr. tunes, Freebirds burritos, and cans of Cactus Cooler.

Their early collaborations included amateur theater productions, ill-fated double-dates, harrowing road trips, and epic dinner parties. These soirees were the seed of their culinary partnership, and continue to this day. Weeks are spent devising and preparing themed parties, which have ranged from A Pirate Feast to a 20-Course Chinese Banquet. Their dress code simply reads, "elastic."

When not near their stoves, Howie and Greg can likely be found eating their way across China. For this insatiable pair, going out for some Sichuan usually involves a trans-Pacific flight. Want to share in their culinary adventures? Visit them on @HowieAndGreg.